Astrology Considered: A Thinking Person's Guide

Compiled and published
by Astrology News Service

Funding for production of this book provided by:
The Urania Trust and the Catharine and Ernest Grant Trust

ISBN: 978-0-692-28413-1

Cover artwork: P. Piner
Cover design: David Lembeck
Production: Kris Brandt Riske

Published by:
Astrology News Service (ANS)
834 S. Arlington Heights Road
Arlington Heights IL 60005

www.astrologynewsservice.com

Printed in the United States of America

Acknowledgements

Publication of this book was made possible by grants from the Urania Trust, a UK astrological educational charity located in London; and the Grant Trust, an educational trust created by Ernest and Catharine Grant, founders of the American Federation of Astrologers (AFA). It's especially gratifying to receive support from two outstanding charitable groups that share a common commitment to advancing astrology in the current era.

The articles and news features you'll find in this collection were written and/or edited by volunteer members the Astrology News Service (ANS) Editorial Board, a group that includes Managing Editor Edward Snow, Articles Editor Armand Diaz, Science Editor Robert Currey, Business Editor Grace K. Morris, Copy Editor Frank Piechoski, Events Editor Gloria Star, Social Media guru Samuel F. Reynolds, and Editorial Advisors Linda Furiate, David Railey, Mark Wolz, Donna Page and Omari Martin.

ANS is a not-for-profit organization that is jointly sponsored by leading astrological organizations in the U.S., including the International Society for Astrological Research (ISAR), the National Council for Geocosmic Research (NCGR), the Organization of Professional Astrologers (OPA), the Association For Astrological Networking (AFAN), and AFA. Stellar advice is routinely provided by the ANS Advisory Council, which is comprised of representatives from each of the sponsoring organizations: Christine Arens, AFA; Terry Johnson, AFAN; Dorothy Oja, ISAR; Nina Gryphon, NCGR; and Alice Kashuba, OPA.

The ANS team is especially indebted to the astrologers who either provided articles or shared their insights as expert witnesses in the news features and interviews published in this book. We're grateful to P. Piner and David Lembeck for their outstanding cover artwork and design. And we greatly appreciate the indefatigable efforts of Kris Brandt Riske, who guided the book through production.

You can continue to follow astrological community developments on the ANS website: www.astrologynewsservice.com.

Contents

Preface: Some Critical Distinctions

A college professor once observed that it's possible to be so open-minded your brains fall out. To guard against this potentially calamitous outcome the mind must wall itself against nonsensical ideas that have the power to muddle clear thinking, he warned. It's important to make critical distinctions between the types of evidence that can reasonably be considered and that which flies in the face of common sense assumptions about the way things work in the natural world.

To emphasize the need for intellectual caution the professor clasped his hands tightly to his head in a mocking fashion. It's not clear whether he's trying to keep something from slipping out—or seeping in. But the meaning of the gesture isn't open to interpretation; it's neither healthy nor productive to dabble with ideas that cannot be substantiated by observable facts.

For centuries, well-meaning scientists have argued that logic, reason and the physical evidence (what we know about the way the universe works) all fail to support the astrological premise; no mechanism known to science can plausibly explain how the centuries-old concept might work. Some critics dismiss astrology out-of-hand as hocus pocus, but the light of reason shines more feebly on these arguments today than it once did.

Researchers in disparate fields of scientific inquiry (quantum physics, biology, cosmology and the relatively new field of consciousness studies) have exposed inconsistencies in the mechanistic arguments scientists have been using for centuries to debunk astrology. What cutting-edge scientists are telling us now is that the natural world they're observing doesn't fit existing scientific theories all that well. It's becoming increasingly apparent that ours is not a world of separate things and events but a cosmos that is coherent, connected and *informed* in ways not previously imagined (at least not in recent centuries). Simply put, we're living in a world in which ancient ideas about non-linear cosmic systems are beginning to make more sense; in a world where astrology makes more sense.

The articles and news features published in this three-part collection are from the Astrology News Service (ANS) archives. Believability and astrology's usefulness and value to society are thematically stressed.

Part I

Astrology Considered...

What Astrology Can Do for You

By Steven Forrest

A woman has a baby and is blissful about it. Another one does the same and spends the rest of her life dreaming about how she might have been a ballerina. The same event: having a kid. But only one smiling woman.

Nobody has a generic formula for happiness, at least not one that does the trick for everyone. That's where astrology comes in.

The birth chart (horoscope) stripped to bare bones is simply a description of the happiest, most fulfilling life that's available to you—personally. It spells out a set of strategies you can use to avoid boring routines, bad choices and dead ends. It lists your resources. And it talks about how your life looks when you're missing the resources and distorting the strategies—shooting yourself in the foot, in other words.

All from a map of the sky?

It's hard to believe, but think for a minute…

"How can the planets possibly affect us? They're millions of miles away," you say.

Astrology's critics are fond of rolling out that argument. But it doesn't hold water. Go out and gaze at the moon. What's really happening? Incomprehensible energies are plunging across a quarter million miles of void, crashing through your eyeballs and creating electrochemical changes in your brain. We call this process "seeing the moon." Certainly planets affect us. The question is where do we draw the boundaries around those effects?

Let's go a step further.

Open your eyes on a starry night. What do you see? A vast, luminous space, full of shadows and light. Now close your eyes so tight they ache. Where are you now? What do you see? Again, a vast, luminous space, full of shadows and light. Consciousness and cosmos are structured around the same laws, follow the same patterns, and even feel pretty much the same to our senses.

"As above, so below." Just as the starry night awes us with its vastness, there's something infinitely deep inside you, a place where you go when you close your eyes, a place that is beyond being an Aries or a Gemini or even a specific gender. At the most profound level, a birth chart is a map back to that magical center. It describes a series of earthly experiences which, if you're brave and open enough, will trigger certain states of consciousness in you—states that operate like powerful spiritual catalysts, vaulting you into higher levels of being.

You are a mysterious being in a mysterious cosmos. You're here for just a little while, a blink of God's eye. You face a monumental task: figuring out what's going on! In that spiritual work, astrology is your ally.

How will it help? Certainly not by pigeon-holing you as a certain "type."

Astrology works by reminding you who you are, by warning you about the comforting lies we all tell ourselves, and by illuminating the experiences that trigger your most explosive leaps in awareness.

After that, the rest is up to you.

Astrology's Unique and Lonely Position in Human Thought

By Grant Lewi (1902–1951)

Astrology maintains a unique and lonely position in human thought. It is "believed in" by a lot of people who know practically nothing about it; and it is "disbelieved in" by even more who know absolutely nothing about it.

Of no other art or science can this be said.

Astronomy, the haughty scientific offspring of astrology, has developed through the centuries into a science of celestial measurement. It has developed even further than the lay mind can comprehend, into a sort of metaphysics of time, space and motion, which only initiates can talk about, let alone comprehend.

Only the most stubborn and bigoted skeptic would think of standing up and saying, for example, that he did not "believe in" the Einstein theory, which is the most abstruse boundary to which astronomical and mathematical philosophy has reached. Such a skeptic would be promptly, and rightly, reprimanded by a more reasonable person, who would remind him that he was unequipped by information either to believe in, or disbelieve in, the Einstein theory.

Similarly, few will be found who have the temerity to "disbelieve" in the law of gravity, Avogadro's hypothesis, Newton's laws of motion, the multiplication table, the effect of sugar injected into the spinal column. These are not matters to believe in or "disbelieve in," but things to know about. Once you know, it is not necessary to believe; they are verifiable by experiment, and subject thereafter to the workings of law.

Astrology's position in human thoughts develops from the fact that it is frequently the subject of the most violent controversy, militantly carried on in the presence of practically no knowledge whatsoever.

Ask your doctor, for example, if he believes in astrology. Ten to one he will shake his head deprecatingly and say, "Of course not!" If you ask him "Why not?" he will probably eye you suspiciously and reply something like, "Don't tell me that an intelligent person like you believes in astrology!"

Just Wondering?

At this point you must avow that you do not believe in astrology, you just were wondering about it. Thereupon, if he runs true to form, he will launch into a long discussion of why astrology must, on the face of it, be nonsense.

He will admit that, once upon a time, most of the world believed in astrology, but that was long ago, in the heyday of ignorance, before the dawn of science and the systematic search for truth. He will point out that astrology believes that the fate of men can be read in the stars; and he will go into a fine frenzy of righteous indignation that any modern could even consider such poppycock.

Listen carefully to everything he says. See if you can detect one sound, scientific reason or proof that astrology is false. See if you can discover, among all the people you can find who "don't believe" in astrology, anyone who has a scientific or even a logical reason for not believing.

Three chief reasons are generally advanced for not believing in astrology. (1) This is not a superstitious age; therefore we should not believe in astrology. (2) It is perfectly ridiculous to believe that the planets can influence human beings. What! Those things millions of miles away? Why it's absurd! (3) The Great Wizard Magipocus read my horoscope at a summer resort, and it was all wrong.

These are virtually all the arguments you will hear on the subject, so let's look at them closely.

(1) It is superstitious because it was believed in a superstitious age, etc. The great principles of mathematics and physics, none of them false, were laid down in an age of the world's youth and "superstition." Large portions of the materia medica were discovered by the ancients. The advanced astronomy of the Egyptians and Babylonians is well known; their calculations have been proved of phenomenal accuracy. These same intellectual and accurate ancients believed in astrology: surely this should be no part of the argument against it! The beliefs and findings of these same ancients, which co-existed with their belief in astrolog, and which have since been given the benefit of modern verification, has been proved amazingly true. It is plainly illogical to dub astrology ipso facto false because it was evolved by those same ancients who gave us the beginnings of astronomy, mathematics, physics, navigation, chemistry and medicine.

(2) It is perfectly ridiculous to believe that the planets could influence us! Now nothing, in itself, is "perfectly ridiculous to believe"—except something that goes against a known law of nature. In fact, all the laws we have of the solar system, with which astrology is concerned, tell us that it is quite illogical that every body of the exerts a measurable, if small, influence on every other body. Thus, it is not "perfectly ridiculous" at all to believe that the planets affect us. It is perfectly ridiculous to believe anything on faith alone, but it is equally ridiculous to disbelieve on un-faith alone. Both faith and un-faith must bow before knowledge, of which, alas, woefully few people have any where astrology is concerned.

(3) Astrology must be false because so many astrologers are fakers. Well, if this were so, the law would be false because many lawyers are crooked; and medicine would be false because so many doctors are quacks and fee splitters. Architecture would be false because the Tower of Pisa leans; and art would be false because Diego Rivera painted Lenin instead of J.P. Morgan in Rockefeller Center.

There are many poor astrologers. There are many people reading and selling horoscopes who are not astrologers at all, but promoters, hack writers and petty racketeers. Yet this argument, like 1 and 2, is a phony, as any logical person can see.

The Smoke of Prejudice

Now in pointing out that all these arguments (the classics generally used against astrology) are not really arguments at all, I have not, of course, proved the truth of astrology. Far from it. I have merely tried to clear away the smoke of prejudice and confusion in order that we may examine the subject on its own merits. It is the fashion today not to believe in astrology, just as long ago it was the fashion to believe in it.

Yet today, or yesterday, or tomorrow, intelligent people neither believe nor disbelieve something of which they are in total ignorance. When such a subject crosses their mind, they say, "I don't know anything about it, and therefore can't have an opinion." Then they are in a proper frame of mind to learn about it and thus acquire, not an opinion, or a belief, but a body of knowledge, from which the truth may appear.

My reasons for "believing in" astrology are extremely simple. I have studied it. I have put together known facts of people's lives with known planetary influences, and I have watched these laws operate in the lives of individuals—of clients, of those close to me, of great men whose biographies are known or whose stories appear from day to day in the press of the contemporary world. I have watched Hitler and his chart, Roosevelt, Mussolini, Stalin; studied the careers and charts of Napoleon, Bismark, the old Kaiser, Lincoln, Washington, Wilson; as well as thousand of lesser individuals who, like yourself, respond to planetary action quite as much as do the great, the near-great, and the pseudo-great who for better and for worse make the headlines. The response of human beings to planetary stimuli is among the most amazing of all the natural phenomena capable of being observed.

I "believe in" astrology for the same reasons you "believe in" the multiplication table or the intoxicating effect of alcohol. It works!

What Astrology Is—and Isn't

By Dorothy Oja

Many people actually think that astrology is the Sun-sign columns found in almost every newspaper and online news media sites. Nothing could be further from the truth. That's not astrology, that's entertainment, which is what is often stated in the fine print beneath astrology columns. Unfortunately, sun-sign columns are one of the most persistently misleading representations of astrology. An amazing fact, however, is that nearly all people know what their Sun-sign is, and more than 31% of the public give some credence to astrology according to a 2008 Harris poll. In 2001, the National Science Foundation concluded that 41 percent of those surveyed believed that astrology is at least somewhat scientific.

So, if astrology isn't Sun-sign columns, then what is it?

"Astrology can tell you what, when, where, and how. However, something else will have to tell you why."—Dr. Joseph (Deepak) Vidmar.

Astrology's Ancient Roots

Astrology is inextricably interwoven throughout our social and cultural history. In fact, it's part of the soul of culture—every museum, every city, in either its buildings or monuments has some Zodiacal representation. Museums the world over hold evidence in artifacts of the value society has placed on astrological symbolism since the earliest times of human history. Some remarkable physical remnants also remain, the most notable being Stonehenge in England, said to have been constructed in phases between 3,000 to 2,000 BCE. It may have had several functions, as a healing and sacred burial site, and also as a huge clock or celestial observatory to measure the Sun's movement and interaction with the Earth, enabling its designers to precisely predict eclipses, solstices, equinoxes and other major celestial events.

Astrology initially developed as a symbolic language for understanding and managing various natural phenomena for agricultural purposes, and to elicit meaning from the contradictions of life. Observing celestial cycles, (most obviously the Moon traveling through its phases monthly) established early on the recognition that there is an inexorable link between the environment around us (including the space above us) and the patterns of our daily lives.

Real astrology is a much more complex process than the simplicity of sun-sign columns. Natal astrology, for example, involves a map of the sky at the time, place, and date of one's birth. It includes analysis of a minimum of 10 celestial bodies and several other mathematical points derived from the calculations of one's birth data. The logic behind this is that we are all influenced by the environments into which we are born, both physical and social.

Astrological Symbols Explained

Dane Rudhyar, one of the most respected astrologers of the 20th century, now deceased, brilliantly explained astrological principles in this article from *Horoscope* magazine 1971:

"More simply stated: the astrologer observes the interrelated motions of the closest factors in the cosmic environment of a particular locality on the earth's surface—i.e., the ten astrological planets—and having identified these planets with the most basic functions and drives in the total organism of a particular human being, he deduces from the interrelationships of the planets at a particular time what the interrelationships between the constituent parts of this human being will be...

"In other words, ten variables are considered sufficient to interpret and to attribute meaning to all past and present events and personal crises and to enable the astrologer to predict future developments. Moreover, the relatively simple formula which a birth-chart constitutes is said by the astrologer to define the very character of the "native"—even though human character is quite a complex affair! Obviously, it can only do so if the ten variables represent the basic qualities of existence which may manifest at any and all levels of human personality.

"We, therefore, are leaving altogether the scientific realm of quantitative measurements and in astrology we are operating in terms of the organic interplay between universal qualities or life rhythms. Each of these ten qualities—modified by their positions within frames of reference like zodiacal signs and natal houses—must, therefore, cover a multitude of cases.

"Astrology deals with individual persons; it is meant to help these persons to live a more harmonious and significant, a richer and fuller life. In pursuit of such a goal, quantitative factors are of little value, for what is at stake is the quality of each of the persons' ten basic bio-psychic organic functions—the Sun function, the Moon function, the Mercury function, the Venus function, the Mars function, etc.

"The specific genius of astrology resides in the astrologer's ability to relate every trait of character, every mode of behavior, every form of intelligence, every vital feeling-response to merely ten variables. The more complex human existence becomes, the more each of those variables has to be loaded with possible meaning—a process which seems to be in direct opposition to the ever more refined type of analysis developed by modern scientists so specialized that indeed they come to know more and more about less and less."

Rudhyar clearly expresses what all astrologers know so well, that there are as many ways of measuring as there are of understanding phenomenon. The scientific, mechanistic way is not the only one, even though it professes to be and appears to have a firm grasp on modern society—I sense this loosening, as the times we are in demand that we take a deeper look at our place in the universe and what we have been led to believe.

It is the distinction and definition of measuring which caused astrology to lose its place of previous honor during the so called Age of Enlightenment, the seventeenth and eighteenth centuries, when the concept of a relationship to the divine or a holistic world view was seen by scientists as associated with religion and therefore rejected by the rise of scientific measurements. The words, astrologer and astronomer were one and the same until the advent of mechanistic science in the seventeenth century. After all, it was Galileo, an astrologer, who rocked the world with his theory, proven true, that the Sun was the center of the solar system and not the Earth. He was imprisoned for that discovery and made by the Catholic Church to recant it.

Astrology is a symbolic language and a testament to our humanity as it seeks not to divide but to harmonize and holistically understand the entire system we live within (earth and cosmos) and not only select parts.

The Science and Astrology Debate

By Edward Snow

The late Arthur M. Young was a mathematician, physicist, engineer, inventor, philosopher and astrologer whose life's work included notable accomplishments in both physics and metaphysics. He was, for example, the inventor of the Bell helicopter. But he also was founder of the Institute for the Study of Consciousness in Berkeley, California.

Mr. Young once noted that in the three hundred years since the Copernican revolution, when science got its start in Galileo's and Newton's discoveries of the laws that account for the motion of the planets, science has repeatedly revised its theories to accommodate new discoveries or facts. In the pattern that has emerged over centuries, science has progressed by revising its beliefs, not by insisting on them.

Examples abound. Although his claims met with initial resistance, Edwin Hubble's discovery that the universe is expanding marked the cosmological end for the almost universally accepted "steady state" theory. And earlier in the 20th century, Max Plank's major finding that light was radiated in "quanta" or units of action, such that their energy divided by the frequency was always the same, was not generally accepted for more than two decades. However, once again, theory was forced to yield to facts.

Quantum theory, which recognizes uncertainty, replaced the determinism of classical theory.

Find Sufficient Evidence

The Institute for the Study of Consciousness founded by Arthur Young remains philosophically committed to the idea that science (and our concept of universe) should not be exclusively limited to that which can be physically measured. Young studied astrology for many years and once made the point that thoughtful people who study the subject find sufficient evidence for its validity. Despite a lack of quantitative precision comparable to some science, there is general agreement among those who practice astrology that they can employ the same rules and get the same results.

Art Young was not content to leave it at that. He also suggested that since the objection of science to astrology is theoretical (astrology could not be true because there is no explanation for it) it must eventually follow that the facts of astrology would win out and make it necessary for science to revise its theories, as has happened so often before.

How likely is this?

Astrology is in the unenviable position of having once been "disproved" by science based on a simple but profound discovery: the planets and even more distant stars are a lot farther from earth than once believed. In fact, the distances are so great that no mechanism known to science (gravity, electromagnetic energy, etc.) could account for the discipline's curious claims, or so it seemed. But then along came the next major scientific revelations and with them festering doubts.

It was bad enough that quantum physics was able to demonstrate that in the unseen world of particle physics every subatomic particle knows what every other subatomic particle it has ever interacted with is doing no matter how great the distance between them becomes. Once subatomic particles become entangled (bump into each other) the simple act of measuring a particle at one location will instantaneously produce a response in its "correlated" pair. The particle twin might be sitting in the lab next door or embedded in surface dust on the dark side of the moon. Or it could be floating aimlessly somewhere in the Oort Cloud; it doesn't matter. If something causes an entangled particle in one location to spin in a certain direction its entangled particle twin will instantaneously spin in the opposite direction.

Spooky Action-at-a-Distance

This phenomenon, which Einstein called "spooky action-at-a-distance," provided spectacular physical evidence that the cosmos is interconnected in ways not previously imagined. And then, as the 20th century was drawing to a close, cosmologists began to converge on the idea that most of the universe is comprised of mysterious dark matter and energy.

That the universe contains more than the physical matter we can see and measure was first suggested by Swiss astrophysicist Fritz Zwicky in 1934. However, his idea was ridiculed and corroborating evidence didn't begin to turn up for another 40 years. Today, cosmologists mostly agree that unseen dark matter and dark energy are what's holding galaxies together in tight clusters while expanding the fabric of space.

Although no one knows what either is, according to some estimates these invisible forces are believed to account for about 90 percent of everything in existence. Among other things, what this would appear to suggest is that the formidable scientific case against astrology is solely based on the 10 percent of reality that can actually be measured by the tools of man. Which, by scientific standards, is a relatively paltry sample size upon which to hang one's hat.

So is it possible that astrology will win out and science will revise its opinions on the subject anytime soon?

It will probably take more than dark matter, dark energy and "spooky action-at-a- distance" to cause a seismic correction in scientific thinking on the subject. But this doesn't change the fact that, in the current era, cutting-edge research continues to expose serious flaws in the physical arguments scientists have used for centuries to debunk astrology. Simply, as methodologies and technologies have improved, researchers have been finding that few of the interesting new things they're able to observe in the natural world fit existing scientific theories all that well. Increasingly, the evidence reveals a cosmos that is more coherent, connected and "informed" in ways not previously imagined.

Of course, none of this necessarily "proves" the validity of astrology; kicking the props from under dated scientific arguments is only the first step in a process. But it's also true that many of the new revelations occurring in the fields of physics, biology, cosmology and the new field of consciousness research are more fundamentally compatible with basic astrological assumptions than some would have us believe.

Some Philosophical Thoughts on a Complex Subject

By Adrian Duncan

It is in the nature of things that nobody can be sure of what "reality" is. What we think of as reality is a consensus of opinions that we subscribe to and are in general agreement on. Our perception of what is going on is completely dominated by our sensory apparatus, and subsequently warped by our opinions.

It may be difficult to accept, but what we think of as going on outside our bodies—and even inside them—is a complex construction entirely subjective in nature. We gravitate toward family, friends and colleagues, sharing our opinions and absorbing theirs, thereby completing the web of illusion that makes up our daily lives.

Our body of opinion that has shaped our experience of reality over the last few hundred years is scientific materialism, which is directly concerned with the perception and measurement of the objective world. Instruments have been developed of greater and greater sensitivity to measure more and more subtle effects. When a new force is perceived and measured, it seems to have philosophical repercussions, which slowly sift down through society, until the fabric of collective consciousness is subtly reconstituted.

Perhaps this is due to the vocabulary that invention generates. When Newton's laws of motion were expounded, the vocabulary of push, pull. Leverage, attraction, action and reaction became a way for us to represent reality, and these laws and words spawned a mechanistic view of understanding nature.

While Newton's heritage was a vocabulary of gravity Einstein's was a vocabulary of light and of relativity that has profoundly reshaped collective consciousness. Relatively sounded the death knell for scientific materialism because it made experience of the object dependent on the perception of the subject. Subject and object are a continuum. And just as subject and object are interrelated so too are body and mind, and matter and energy—with consciousness free to dwell at any point on this duality spectrum. Where before the whole crux of scientific investigation was to be as detached as possible from the object, relativity theory has shown this to be an ineffective and inaccurate means of investigating subtle nonmaterial forces.

Where Astrology Comes In…

This is where astrology comes in as a tool for perceiving reality. Dealing more with the mind and senses of the subject, or individual, there is an intrinsic acceptance that the object—that individual's experience—is mutually interrelated and interdependent. Rather than life simply happening to us we are constantly evoking events in a complex dance between our character and our fate, or between our consciousness and the object of our consciousness.

An astrological consultation I once gave may serve to illustrate this phenomenon. It was for a middle-aged lady who had a very tenuous grasp of reality, with powerful delusions about being followed by men. I did my best to persuade her that she was probably imagining most of the incidents, based on the astrological fact that she had the astrological sign Pisces rising on the ascendant (where the sun comes up in the East) and the planet Neptune on the descendant (where it sets in the West). In astrology speak, Neptune is the planetary "ruler" of Pisces and has been negatively identified with illusion and delusional patterns of behavior. Simply, this particular configuration might be expected to evoke a tendency for the woman to be confused in her relationships with others if other elements of the birth chart confirmed this possibility.

It was an unconvincing consultation undermined by my inability to deal with her mental state. A few minutes after she left my office I decided to go out shopping but on opening the door I found the lady on the stairs studying a bus timetable and muttering to herself. Not wishing to appear to be following her, I smiled weakly and retired to my office, waiting until she had proceeded on her way.

Acutely aware that I might confirm her fantasies if I crossed her path I walked into town using a circuitous route. Twenty minutes later I arrived in the town square and as I did so the bus pulled up alongside me and my client stepped out. She took one startled look at me and started walking rapidly in the other direction.

Experience had vindicated my client and proved to her that her version of reality was the correct one. The extraordinary thing was that my own behavior had been altered, and events had conspired to bring about that which I had wanted to avoid. This scenario plays out in all our lives as our personal character stamps its impression on a reality that is constantly adjusting to who we are and what we do.

The corollary of this is good news in terms of free will. By adapting our behavior, we can alter reality and our experience of it. And everything in our world will alter in it, including the people we relate to.

Herein lays the power of astrology, which can be released by judicious work with the energies reflected in the horoscope. And herein lies the possibility of transformation.

Two Blind Men Groping the Cosmic Elephant

By Robert Gover

I view the difference between the scientific and astrological perceptions of the cosmos as akin to the proverbial blind men groping the elephant, each describing what he'd found and hotly arguing with others who are describing different parts of the same elephant.

This gives me a pinch of sympathy for the likes of scientist Richard Dawkins who debunk astrology as primitive superstition and utter nonsense because it does not agree with the part of the cosmic elephant science has hold of.

But what Dawkins and other debunkers usually mean by "astrology" are those Sun sign blurbs in newspapers. Most astrologers agree that Sun sign astrology is ridiculous. What sign or constellation the Sun was in when you were born is but one aspect of a full astrological reading. And many, if not most Sun sign blurbs are conjured by supposing everyone born with the sun in a given sign took their first breath as the sun was peeking over the horizon at 0 degrees of that sign—a ridiculous assumption.

In this regard, debunkers of astrology are like a flock of crows perched on a telephone line, eyeing a field of corn that is "guarded" by a bunch of straw propped up by a stick and dressed to appear as a human. Their angry chatter is about a scarecrow version of astrology.

Precession Is Old News

Then there are the debunkers who proclaim that modern western astrologers are wrong because of the procession of the equinoxes. The precession means that our map of the zodiac changes by one degree every 71.6 years. This in turn means that everyone's sun sign is really regressed by 24 degrees after 2,000 years. Those born with, say, Sun in Sagittarius really have Sun in the previous sign, Scorpio. Scorpios are really Libras, and so forth around the zodiac.

But astrologers have been keenly aware of the precession for the past 2,000 years or more. Mayan mathematicians calculated it with much more precision than any others, and ancient Hindu Vedic astrologers have based their charts on it for centuries.

And there is more to the precession than the apparent backward movement of the constellations and/or signs of the zodiac that appear to surround our solar system. The telescopes of modern astronomy have taken us into the vastness beyond and shown us a fury of cosmic activity.

"Our Milky Way Galaxy has two distinct parts in its outer reaches that rotate in opposite directions. According to a report posted on the space.com website, the galaxy has a bulbous core where stars are tightly packed and orbiting rather furiously around the central black hole. Then there's the big flat disk with its spiral arms, also orbiting the galactic center somewhat in the manner of a hurricane's spiral bands. We live on one of those arms. Around it all is a halo of stars that don't all behave in such an orderly fashion. The astrological signs map "neighborhoods" in the cosmos. These extend so far beyond our solar system that it is hard to imagine. Used as geocentric maps, and taking into consideration the mysterious goings-on in galaxies so distant we have yet to find them, the ancient astrological signs continue to serve their purpose. This is especially so when we keep the focus on what's happening within our own tiny solar system.

Western astrology is sometimes called "seasonal" for it calculates based on the four seasons, the two equinoxes and the two solstices. If we calculate according to the precession, in just over a couple of thousand of years from now the sun will line up with the *constellation* of Capricorn around the time of the spring equinox in the northern hemisphere. But when the sun reaches the spring equinox degree in Aries each year, it's the end of winter that we experience. So it's really a question of which perspective we choose. We can calculate our position according to the precession of the equinoxes, or we can calculate it according to the seasons of the year as we experience them.

A "Dwarf" in Name Only

Debunkers also denigrate astrology because there is no known "medium" or cause-effect mechanism for why the planets influence us. Astrologers agree: No one knows why there is a correlation between what goes on "up there" and "down here." The ancient astrological saying, "As above, so below" captures this observed synchronicity. No one has discovered why or how such influences work. Gravity? Certainly not. Pluto—so small it was downgraded by astronomers to a "dwarf planet"—is so distant from the sun, and its orbit so idiosyncratic that its history of coinciding with major turning points when forming certain angles has no other explanation except that offered by the astrological paradigm.

Although planets repeatedly form primary angles to each other—the most frequent being the phases of the Sun and Moon—they do so in an ever-changing celestial context. Every new Moon occurs with the other bodies of the cosmos arranged differently than the last new Moon. The modern scientific method relies on duplication of results. From an astrological perspective, history repeats but does not duplicate. No two moments in cosmic time are ever the same.

A new perspective on astrology arrived with the rise of the uncertainty principle, quantum physics, which also overturned some long-standing beliefs of Newtonian physics, or what some call "the old science." Quantum physicists found something very curious happening in the subatomic cosmos: every subatomic particle knows what every other subatomic particle it has ever interacted with is doing no matter how great the distance between them becomes. Each responds to the other's changes. This interaction of subatomic particles is as mysterious as our interaction with the planets. No one yet knows why, or what cause-effect mechanism is at work in either realm.

This mystery also connects with the ancient astrological saying, "As above, so below." Both the cosmos and the subatomic realm hold secrets yet to be unlocked. What we know about both is that there is some kind of interaction taking place. What we don't know is how these interactions operate. Yet, just as quantum physicists can count on certain subatomic results, so astrologers can count on certain planetary cycles coinciding with the same kinds of events they repeatedly coincided with in the past.

For instance, every time Saturn (strictures, established systems, protector of the status quo) has arrived in mid-Capricorn and simultaneously formed a 90-degree angle to another of the outermost planets moving through Aries, the nation has experienced a great depression: the 1930s, 1870s and 1840s. The most indicative angles formed by the planets are conjunctions (when two or more planets are within 10 degrees of each other as seen from Earth), 90-degree squares, 180-degree oppositions and 270-degree squares.

Pluto in Capricorn

Every approximately 248 years when Pluto's orbit returns it to Capricorn, major cultural restructurings or revolutions have occurred. This is so going back to the Roman times, the last two times being in the late 1700s (American and French revolutions) and the early 1500s (discovery of gold and silver in the Americas). This suggests that the astrological belief that Saturn "rules" Capricorn is valid.

We are now moving through another time of Pluto in Capricorn (2008 to 2023) and during much of this 25-year period, Pluto will form a 90-degree square angle to Uranus in Aries. This will put Pluto opposite the U.S. natal Sun in Cancer. Since the U.S. Sun is square the U.S. Saturn in Libra, and Libra is opposite Aries, Uranus will be simultaneously opposite the U.S. Saturn. The "transit-to-natal" pattern thus formed is what astrologers call a grand cross. It can be counted on to bring tremendous and long-lasting changes in all dimensions of our earthly experience.

Astrology cannot predict exactly what will change how, but it's possible to deduce some pending changes from the thrust of current events, and what systems in human affairs have gotten out of balance. Economically, the gap between the super wealthy few and the rest of humanity has never been greater. This suggests that the kind of revolts taking place in the Middle East and the U.S. Midwest in early 2011 are likely to spread and intensify as this aspect tightens to exact by 2015.

Most debunkers of astrology have hung a "do not disturb" sign on the door of their beliefs. If they were to examine astrology on its own terms, they would find that this part of the mysterious cosmic elephant helps define other parts.

New Academic Movement Champions Astrology

By Edward Snow

They scoffed at Sigmund Freud's disturbing ideas about repressed libidinal impulses and childhood sexuality, and didn't think much of the psychiatrist's preoccupation with dream analysis, either.

But despite his more exaggerated claims and unsubstantiated theories, Freud's psychoanalytic method—and its many offshoots in the wider field of depth psychology—is currently viewed by Western scholars as "a necessary corrective to the values and world view of the nineteenth century."

Writing in *Archai: The Journal of Archetypal Cosmology*, editor Keiron Le Grice places Freud in a unique category of visionaries who serve as emissaries for emerging truths that become a lightning rod for dismissive skeptical criticism and contempt.

In Freud's day, the "shockingly wicked" notion that humans might be the unwitting instrument of unconscious impulses and complexes was met with derision and scorn. In the current century, Le Grice sees a parallel in the response that has greeted the emergence of a controversial new academic discipline that is based on the methodology, interpretive principles and cosmological perspective of astrology, the "most controversial subject of all."

The new discipline draws upon an understanding of archetypal patterns described in psychology, history, art and culture by Carl Jung, James Hillman, Joseph Campbell and others, he noted.

"Although many are quick to reject the truth claims of astrology, striking evidence of correlations between planetary cycles and the major patterns of world history has given archetypal astrology a new, unexpected credibility. There is compelling evidence that astrology is once again worthy of serious consideration," he maintains.

Le Grice says the new academic discipline is based on research begun at the Esalen Institute in Big Sur, Calif., in the 1970s. A detailed account is provided by cultural historian and philosopher Richard Tarnas in his award-winning book, *Cosmos and Psyche: Intimations of a New World View.*

Challenging Establishment Views

Like Vienna, Le Grice says the San Francisco Bay Area has become a hotbed for challenging embedded establishment views on why humans behave the way they do. The movement currently involves a group of about 70 researchers, practitioners and scholars who have come together to form the Archetypal Research Collective. The group seeks to understand, in philosophical and scientific terms, the basis for astrological correlations. And it hopes to bring the work of Tarnas and like-minded academics to the attention of a wider audience, he said.

Tarnas studied cultural history and depth psychology at Harvard, earned a PhD in philosophy from the Saybrook Institute in San Francisco, and worked and lived for more than 10 years at Esalen Institute in Big Sur, Calif., at one point serving as the Institute's director of programs and education. He is founding director of the graduate program in Philosophy, Cosmology and Consciousness at the California Institute of Integral Studies (CIIS) in San Francisco, where he currently teaches, and also is on the faculty at the Pacifica Graduate Institute in Santa Barbara, Calif. *The Passion of the Western Mind*, his best-selling history of Western thought, is currently used as a textbook by more than 100 universities around the world.

The scholarly academic began to develop a rigorous way to test the planetary themes and qualities described by traditional astrology while working at Esalen with psychologist Stanislav Grof, one of the founders of transpersonal psychology. The pair was studying the timing and character of transformational experiences when it was suggested they should check out astrology.

After getting beyond initial skepticism, the pair examined hundreds and eventually thousands of individual astrological charts, concluding that the archetypal principles astrologers associate with the sun, moon and planets—and the correlations between planetary motion and events on earth they uncovered—were "undeniable and uncanny in their subtlety and specificity."

According to Le Grice, the central supposition informing archetypal astrology is that one can gain a deep insight into the archetypal dynamics underlying human experience by interpreting the meaning of the positions of the planets in relationship to each other. Importantly, Tarnas and Grof were able to demonstrate that the angular relationships formed between transiting planets affected not only the personal biographies of individuals but the changing patterns of collective human experience as well.

Historical Evidence

In *Cosmos and Psyche*, Tarnas describes how astrology illuminated key moments in the lives of pivotal historical figures in the West. For example, when Galileo wrote the *Starry Messenger*, a defining moment in the birth of the modern era, the transiting planet Uranus, which is archetypically associated with revolutionary breakthroughs and awakenings, was forming a particularly powerful one-time configuration in his birth chart.

The same type of configuration or "aspect" was influencing the birth chart of Rene Descartes in 1637 when he published his epoch-defining *Discourse on Methods*, and was prominent in the birth chart of Isaac Newton in 1687 when he published the *Principia*, which is widely regarded as the foundational work of modern science. Freud's psychoanalytic theory, Einstein's theory of relativity and Darwin's theory of natural selection also emerged in coincidence with the same planetary cycle.

Le Grice believes Tarnas and Grof succeeded in presenting the astrological perspective in a radically different light, finding in the long-discredited ancient symbolic system something of great value to the postmodern mind. Potentially, he thinks that something could "radically transform our understanding of the nature of the universe itself."

An Introduction to Archetypal Astrology

By Richard Tarnas

A birth chart or natal chart is a portrait of the heavens at the moment of one's birth. The Sun, Moon and planets are positioned around the chart to reflect their positions around the Earth when one was born. For example, where the symbol for the Sun is located in the chart reflects the time of day one was born: thus, if one were born at noon, the Sun would be at the top of the chart (called the Midheaven), while if one was born at dawn the Sun would be shown rising on the left side of the chart near the eastern horizon (called the Ascendant).

The main difference between the natal chart and the astronomical reality it portrays is that the natal chart has two dimensions rather than three, and it does not reflect the varying distances of the planets from the Earth. What the birth chart does convey is the exact pattern of angular relationships existing between the planets and the Earth at the time and place of one's birth. The basic principle of astrology is that the planets have a fundamental, cosmically based connection to specific archetypal forces or principles which influence human existence, and that the patterns formed by the planets in the heavens bear a meaningful correspondence to the patterns of human affairs on the Earth. In terms of individuals, the positions of the planets at the time and place of a person's birth are

regarded as corresponding to the basic archetypal patter
life and character.

Astrology makes possible a further understanding of one's life—
its ups and downs, the crises and the breakthroughs, the periods of major change and transformation—through the study of transits. Transits occur when the planets currently in the sky form certain geometrical patterns with respect to the planetary positions at one's birth. The nature of those patterns—which planets are involved and how they are positioned—appears to correlate in a strikingly consistent way with the archetypal character of the experiences one tends to have at that time.

Three Primary Issues

To begin, I would like to address three important matters that people usually need discussed when approaching astrology. The first concerns the nature of archetypes, the second involves the question of determinism vs. free will, and the third concerns the nature of astrology's causal mechanism, or why it works. These three issues are closely interrelated.

First, what is an archetype? Archetypes can be understood and described in many ways, and in fact much of the history of Western thought from Plato and Aristotle onward has been concerned with this very question. But for our present purposes, we can define an archetype as a universal principle or force that affects—impels, structures, permeates—the human psyche and human behavior on many levels. One can think of them as primordial instincts, as Freud did, or as transcendent first principles as Plato did, or as gods of the psyche as James Hillman does.

Archetypes (for example Venus or Mars) seem to have a transcendent mythic quality, yet they also have very specific psychological expressions—as in the desire for love and the experience of beauty (Venus) or the impulse towards forceful activity and aggression (Mars). Moreover, archetypes seem to work from both within and without, for they can express themselves as impulses and images from the interior psyche, yet also as events and situations in the external world.

Jung thought of archetypes as the basic constituents of the human psyche, shared cross-culturally by all human beings, and he regarded them as universal expressions of the collective unconscious. Much earlier, the Platonic tradition considered archetypes to be not only psychological but also cosmic and objective, as primordial forms of a Universal Mind that transcended the human psyche. Astrology would appear to support the Platonic view as well as the Jungian, since it gives evidence that Jungian archetypes are not only visible in human psychology, in human experience and behavior, but are also linked to the macrocosm itself—to the planets and their movements in the heavens. Astrology thus supports the ancient idea of an anima mundi, or world soul, in which the human psyche participates. From this perspective, what Jung called the collective unconscious can be viewed as being ultimately embedded within the cosmos itself.

The issue of free will vs. determinism: It used to be believed that astrology revealed a person's destined fate, that the birth chart was rigidly deterministic. Properly understood, however, astrology can serve to greatly increase personal freedom, rather than limit it. Partly this is because awareness of the basic archetypal structures and patterns of meaning in one's birth chart allows one to bring considerably more consciousness to the task of fulfilling one's deepest potential, one's authentic nature. But astrology's emancipatory character also derives from the fact that the more deeply we understand the archetypal forces that affect our lives, the more free we can be in our dealings with them. If we are altogether unconscious of these potent forces, we are like puppets of the archetypes: we then act according to unconscious motivations without any possibility of our being intelligent agents interacting with those forces.

Astrology's Great Merit

To the exact extent that we are conscious of the archetypes, we can respond with greater autonomy and self-awareness. This is of course the whole rationale for depth psychology, from Freud and Jung onward—to become conscious of the unconscious, to release ourselves from the bondage of blind action, to explore and experience the hidden forces in the human psyche. Astrology's great merit is that it seems to reveal very precisely which archetypes are especially important to each person, how they interact with each other, and when and how they are most likely to be expressed in the course of each life.

Related to this issue is the question of our birth, and how random is the fate by which we are assigned something as weighty as the birth chart with its specific configuration of planets. I personally believe that the circumstances of our birth are not accidental, but are in some sense a consequence of our spiritual and karmic character. Like many others, I have come to believe that we choose the circumstances of our lives, we choose the family and culture and age into which we are born, and that this choice is somehow made from a higher level of our spiritual being than that of which we are usually conscious.

From this point of view, the birth chart is not the randomly allotted prison structure of our inexorable fate, but can be seen rather as defining the basic structure of our potential unfolding—suggesting the personal gifts and trials that we have chosen for this lifetime to work with and evolve through. Astrology illuminates the fundamental archetypal dynamics that profoundly condition our lives, which is not to say they absolutely determine our lives. Because our personal response to life always contains an element of unpredictability and potential freedom, and because astrology gives a greater understanding of our basic archetypal complexes and their timing, then a knowledge of our birth chart and transits can significantly increase the range of options, flexibility and intelligence with which we approach life. The study of astrology can be extraordinarily liberating.

Finally, the issue of a causal mechanism, or why astrology works: It seems unlikely to me that the planets send out some kind of physical emanations that causally influence events in human life in a mechanistic way. The range of coincidences between planetary positions and human existence is just too vast, too experimentally complex, too aesthetically subtle and endlessly creative to be explained by physical factors alone. I believe that a more plausible and comprehensive explanation is that the universe is informed and pervaded by a fundamental holistic patterning which extends through ever level, so that a constant synchronicity or meaningful correlations exists between astronomical events and human events. This is represented in the basic esoteric axiom, "as above, so below," which reflects a universe all of whose parts are integrated into an intelligible whole.

From this perspective, the planets themselves are not "causing" anything to be happening in our lives, any more than the hands on a clock are now causing it to be 7:30 PM. Rather, the planetary positions are indicative of the cosmic state of the archetypal forces at that time. The fact that the planets constantly seem to indicate these things with such accuracy simply suggests that the cosmic order is much more profound and pervasive than our conventional beliefs have assumed. But the relationship between a specific planetary pattern and a human experience is best seen as one of meaningful correlation or correspondence, not one of simple linear causality.

There is, however, a sense in which causality does enter into the astrological perspective, and this is the sense of archetypal causation (comparable to Aristotle's concepts of formal and final causes). While the physical planets themselves may bear only a synchronistic connection with a given human experienced, that experience is nevertheless being affected or caused—influenced, patterned, impelled, drawn forth—by the relevant planetary archetypes, and in this sense it is quite appropriate to speak, for example, of Saturn (as archetype) "influencing" one in a specific way, or as "governing" certain kinds of experience.

But why should the cosmos have established a systematic correspondence between planetary patterns and archetypally patterned phenomena in human lives? There are many possible answers to this questions, not the least of which might point toward a kind of intrinsic aesthetic splendor in the universe, an overflow of cosmic intelligence and delight that reveals itself in this continuous marriage of mathematical astronomy and mythic poetry. But in more pragmatic human terms, my sense of astrology is that the constant coincidence between planetary positions and human lives exists as a kind of universal code for the human mind to unravel, so that we can better understand ourselves and our world, rediscover our deep connection to the cosmos, and be more complete human beings.

Celebrity Scientist Shares Views on Cosmos

By Edward Snow

In the opening episode of National Geographic's television series, *Cosmos: A Space Time Odyssey*, program host Neil deGrasse Tyson, an astrophysicist, author and science communicator, shares one of his pet theories. What separates mankind from other creatures on the planet is man's unique ability to recognize patterns in nature, he suggests.

In a charitable spirit, Dr. Tyson urges his national television audience not to be too hard on those ancient observers who looked to the night sky for more than clues about when to plant crops or how to find one's way on land or at sea. Given mankind's penchant for pattern recognition, it's understandable that our distant ancestors might get the idea that planetary patterns forming in the night sky were infused with significance and meaning. However, we now know what the stars and planets are made of and where comets come from. So it's unseemly for moderns to entertain such ideas.

In Dr. Tyson's narrative, science arrived to rescue humanity from the slagheap of medieval mysticism in the 16th century and has expanded our horizons exponentially since then. Today we know our place in the physical universe and it is infinitesimally small. There are an estimated 300 billion stars in our own Milky Way Galaxy, many much larger than our own bright sun. And there are trillions of galaxies similar to our own strung out on web-like filaments over unimaginable distances across the known universe.

Beyond this, the astrophysicist reports there may be many other unseen parallel universes that coexist with our own in a so-called multiverse or meta universe. Purportedly, the unseen multiverse is comprised of everything that exists and can exist: the entirety of space, time, matter and energy as well as the physical laws and constants that describe them. One assumption is that the various parallel universes in the multiverse, if they exist at all, operate with different laws of physics. Most likely, we'll never learn if this is true or not.

Suffice to say, scientists have learned a great deal more about the universe earthlings currently cohabit and it's nothing like anyone envisioned at the start of the 20th century. We're living in an age of discovery like no other with dazzling new space technologies opening our eyes to a dynamic, expanding universe that is constantly on the move and continually reinventing itself.

Out there in space are exploding stars, colliding galaxies and voracious black holes that inspire us to appreciate anew Isaac Newton's Universal Law of Gravitation. The fabric of space is pocked with the remnants of giant burned out stars (black holes) that were formed long ago when the self-same giant stars ran out of nuclear fuel and exploded as a supernova somewhere in space. Common and not-so-common chemical elements created in these explosions were blasted into space as star dust, which ultimately was collected and shaped by gravity into new stars and planets and everything else that can be found on our own and distant worlds.

All We Are is Stardust

Tyson tells us that the calcium in our bones, iron in our blood and all the other elements we know about were forged and fused in stellar explosions that occurred eons ago in far-flung reaches of the galaxy. All we are is stardust, he explains.

It's hard to determine which is more remarkable: the fact we're made of star stuff or the fact humanity had the ingenuity and genius to figure this out. Thanks to modern science we know the dynamic creative process on display in our expanding universe is not unlike the patterns of life, death and renewal scientists notice at every layer of existence. Stars are born, die and are recycled anew as part of a seemingly endless existential drama.

In addition to scattering stardust, when a giant star explodes its core collapses to form a powerful black hole. In these dead zones gravity is so extreme it overwhelms all other forces in the universe. So it is curtains for any near-by sun or stellar gas that strays within the black hole's event horizon. The event horizon establishes a gravitational point of no return; what happens to whatever crosses the line is not reversible.

Tyson tells us there are an estimated 100 million menacing black holes in the Milky Way galaxy alone and an astronomical number residing elsewhere in the universe. He also mentions super-massive black holes that exist at the centers of every galaxy and weigh-in with masses ranging between hundreds of thousands to billions of solar masses. It's not clear which came first, the galaxies or the super-massive black holes. But their formation speaks to the stupefying enormity of creation.

This, in a way, is Dr. Tyson's point in a nutshell. Now that we know the cosmological scale we're dealing with it's obvious how wrong some centuries-old cosmological notions must be. What the science communicator can't seem to figure out is why these dated concepts are still hanging around and gaining currency in the current century? He seems to be genuinely concerned and embarrassed because the good news message about the wonderful achievements of science isn't reaching all ears.

A Different Perspective

Truth is, science and astrology are not mutually exclusive enterprises. People continue to visit astrologers in the modern era because they find the information gleaned to be useful or helpful in some way. And because there are moments when astrology's mind-blowing accuracy impresses. It should be noted that astrologers, more than most, have benefited from the magnificent revolution in optics and imaging technologies that have revolutionized scientific exploration of the solar system. Uniquely, astrologers have been able to bring back to earth the practical fruits of technical astronomical labors

Since the discovery of Uranus in 1781 astrological sleuths in the western world have been on a mission to detect and discern the archetypal energies that apply to newly discovered worlds in the solar system earth calls home. In the process that unfolds, astronomers discover distant celestial objects and members of the astrological community almost immediately begin an informal matching process that seeks to determine where the newcomer fits in the cosmic scheme. At the start, some intuitive guesswork is involved. But the actual investigative method used by astrologers might loosely qualify as an applied science. There's a working hypothesis (suspected characteristics) and a network of astrologers observing and recognizing patterns and informally sharing insights on a global scale. In all of the human event areas addressed by astrology.

Alas, for many in the scientific community some of the subjective investigative methods astrologers use to embroider their ideas don't pass the sniff test. Modern scientists tend to envision themselves on the cutting edge of knowledge and, understandably, value forward leaning momentum. In the worldview blindly embraced, astrology is one of a number of things rational people should have outgrown. There's no reason to go down this road because it's obviously a dead end. Or so they say.

In his role as science communicator Tyson has never been especially kind to astrology or astrologers. He is, for example, the scientist who in one of his books was the first to inform the public there are more than 12 astrological signs in the zodiac. His idea was to mock astrologers as fools incapable of understanding how celestial mechanics work. However, all that was demonstrated with this ruse was the fact the celebrity scientist had not seriously studied the subject and confused stellar constellations with astrological signs. Twelve astrological signs have been the Ptolemaic standard since before the birth of Christ.

A Way Forward

Tyson and other critics of astrology tell the public that astrology has been scientifically tested and found wanting. However, there is glaring contrary evidence suggesting the science side has a lot of work to do before it can reasonably make such claims. To resolve the issue (somewhat) here's a simple test fair-minded critics of astrology might try:

Make an appointment with a qualified professional astrologer and show up with a certified birth certificate that includes date, time, and place of birth. The brave souls who take this on should be prepared to provide the astrologer with the timing (date and place) for an event in their personal life that changed everything for them. It is the astrologer's job to explain and describe how this important event was mirrored in the heavens at the time it occurred. If there's anything to astrology, a truly life-changing event should be reflected in the alignments forming between transiting planets and the placement of planets in the critic's birth map or horoscope. The actionable influences should be obvious to the astrologer and, if properly explained, to the fair-minded critic as well.

Of course, this is not a proper scientific test. But the results might open a few closed eyes.

Actually, experiments like this go on all the time; astrological clients often test the process in this way. In his *Cosmos* TV series Tyson used several minutes of air time to describe an event that changed everything for him when he was a teenager growing up in Brooklyn, New York. Apparently, Tyson was an outstanding 17-year-old high school student whose academic promise earned him an invitation to meet astronomer Carl Sagan at his home and spend the afternoon visiting with him. At the time Sagan was host of the original *Cosmos* TV series. Three decades later Tyson still remembers the exact date of this meeting: December 20, 1975. And he shared this information with his 2014 television audience: "I already knew I wanted to become a scientist," Tyson told *Cosmos* viewers. "But that afternoon I learned from Carl the kind of person I wanted to become."

An Internet bio provides October 5, 1958 as Tyson's date of birth in New York City (no time given). Astrologer and author Anthony Louis observes that on this date transiting Pluto had advanced to the same degree of Libra where Mercury and the Sun reside in Tyson's natal birth chart only seconds of arc apart in the eleventh degree of the sign. When planets are aligned in the same zodiacal degree in a birth chart astrologers call this a conjunction. When a third planet joins the pair by transit a triple conjunction occurs; the transiting planet is said to infuse with or trigger the combination's possibilities. There isn't a scientific explanation for why this happens.

Louis explains that Pluto, the planet of life-altering transformation, is usually active at times when events occur that divide people's lives into before and after sequences. An astrologer noticing this relative rare exact triple conjunction forming in Tyson's birth map would advise him to anticipate a radically transformative experience affecting his sense of identity (Sun) and way of thinking (Mercury) during the time period indicated. Whether this combination indicates a beneficial or more challenging experience largely depends on how other planetary energies are involved at the time.

On the magical day Tyson shared the afternoon with Carl Sagan another transiting planet, Uranus, had advanced to form an exact conjunction with Jupiter's placement in Tyson's natal birth chart. Astrologers would read this as another indication of an extraordinary opportunity; Uranus is linked to cosmology and science and Jupiter with expansive optimism and hope. But, Louis says, Pluto is forming the more significant aspect on this day.

On the astronomy side Pluto has been downgraded and lumped with other dwarf planets in a separate category. In contrast, astrologers see the powerful and transformative planet as a solar system heavyweight and front man for a collection of Oort Cloud ice worlds that are poised to reveal what their impact on the human psyche will be.

Not everyone has the kind of memorable, life-altering experience Tyson described on his TV show. However, whenever the timing for a course-changing event is known, a competent astrologer will know where to look for clues and how to plausibly explain the coinciding astrological symbolism displayed in the heavens at the time.

Are There Really 14 Signs?

By Diana K. Rosenberg

Dr. Neil deGrasse Tyson, research scientist in astrophysics at Princeton and Curator of Astronomy at the Hayden Planetarium of the American Museum of Natural History, has become a familiar face on television; he frequently appears on talk shows, cheerily and with gusto declaiming that astrologers are ignorant of the "fact" that there are fourteen zodiacal constellations, rather than twelve. He has also authored several books, among them *Universe Down to Earth* (Columbia University Press, 1994).

In this work, on page 210 he writes:

"[T]he zodiac contains 14 constellations, not 12. The Sun, after leaving the constellation Scorpius, enters the constellation Ophiuchus. It then stays in Ophiuchus for a longer (emphasis Tyson's) period of time than Scorpius, the sign that is advertised to precede Sagittarius. The confusing conclusion is that most Scorpions are actually Ophiuchans, and all Scorpions and Ophiuchans are currently Librans. The fourteenth constellation in the set is Cetus. It is a large constellation that dips into Pisces. The Sun passes through Cetus briefly as it ambles through Pisces, but you are not normally informed of this in the horoscope pages."

But we are speaking of astrology, and Dr. Tyson knows that astrologers use celestial longitudes; he knows (or should know) that the Sun enters the longitudes of Scorpius and Ophiuchus at the same time, and remains in them for the same length of time. While it is true that the ecliptic runs through part of Ophiuchus, thus rightly making him part of the zodiac, the span of the Serpent-Bearer, in celestial longitude,[1] matches that of the Scorpion, and so he cannot be called a "thirteenth sign!" In actuality, the 8th zodiacal constellation should be called Scorpius/Ophiuchus—indeed, the two figures actually contact each other, as the left foot of Ophiuchus treads upon the Scorpion in order (according to tradition) to crush it. It is this overlap which creates a problem, and makes it seem as though Ophiuchus' allotment of degrees exceeds the Scorpion's.

Tyson wrote that the ecliptic stays in Ophiuchus for a longer period of time than in Scorpius, but this holds true only if the artificial demarcation lines imposed by the IAU in 1930 are adhered to;[2] the astronomers who determined those lines could not bring themselves to accept overlaps or combinations; the lines, they believed, must keep each figure entirely separate, and the sky figures, like caged animals, must remain within them.[3] A quick glance at the lines dividing the Scorpion and the feet of Ophiuchus show that absolutely no allowance was made for the Scorpion's upper half! Ophiuchus' left foot, which is treading upon the Scorpion, is given all; the Scorpion, none. The poor arachnid, already truncated early on in history by losing his claws to form the Scales of Libra, has been further mutilated with the loss of his northern legs!

Here's the real zodiacal story, based on celestial longitude:

The Scorpion's earliest stars[4] are Xi Scorpii in the North Claw, and Delta Scorpii (Dschubba or Isidis) in the forehead, at 1 Sagittarius 18 and 2 Sagittariius 34, respectively.

Ophiuchus' earliest star is Yed Prior, Delta Ophiuchi, at the left hand grasping Serpens, the Serpent, at 2 Sagittarius 18.

The Scorpion's last stars (actually Clusters—the Scorpion's tail lies in the nebulous Milky Way) are Acumen, M7 Scorpii, near the sting and Globular Cluster NGC 6496 below the sting, at 28 Sagittarius 43 and 29 Sagittariius 48.

Ophiuchus' last star is Sinistra, Nu Ophiuchi, at his right hand grasping the Serpent: 29 Sagittarius 45.

Astronomer Confused

Tyson claims that Ophiuchus is longer than Scorpius, but only if you include its outlying, dim stars; and since we are talking zodiac here, note that the first stars of the Sagittarius Archer precede the longitudes of those faint, outlying Ophiuchus stars, thus seizing the zodiacal baton where Scorpius/Ophiuchus hands it off; so the Serpent-Bearer cannot be considered a longer zodiacal figure than Scorpius. The earliest Sagittarius star is variable X Sagittarii at 27 Sagittarius 15—showing that the constellation of the Archer takes its position as the rightful ninth zodiacal figure, precluding any claims of Ophiuchus.

The span of Serpens Cauda (the tail of the Serpent grasped by Ophiuchus) continues into tropical Capricorn—it is this continuance of the Serpent's stars that may have deluded Dr. Tyson into thinking that Ophiuchus himself extends so far (in ancient times they were one figure, called "Serpentarius" or "Ophiuchus vel Serpentarius"—a shamanic figure[5] struggling with the darkly powerful Serpent and at the same time attempting to crush the Scorpion-of-death), but the IAU officially declared them separate constellations, ignoring centuries of knowledge and tradition, even dividing Serpens itself into two entirely separate parts!

And as for the statement that "all Scorpions and Ophiuchans are currently Librans," that's a howler. Apparently Dr. Tyson, in his rush to mix apples and oranges (in this case the sidereal zodiac and the tropical zodiac), has got his head in a twist. Switching from the star figures to the tropical zodiac, one must go forward one sign; what he (apparently) wanted to say was that all Scorpions and Ophiuchans are currently Sagittarians (tropical Sagittarians, that is).[6]

As for Cetus "dipping" into Pisces (a strange description, as Cetus is south of, i.e. below, the Fishes), or for the Sun transiting Cetus (which would make him part of the zodiac—Dr. Tyson's so-called "fourteenth sign"), one look at a star map shows that it just ain't so. The ecliptic does come close (below the cord of the West Fish of Pisces) but nonetheless does stay clear of the Sea-Monster's domain (here the IAU astronomers got it right, taking care to keep the most northerly point of Cetus just below the ecliptic line).[7] Given this, it is hard to understand Dr. Tyson's claim.

Although his purpose is not to enlighten but to mock, we are indebted to the astrophysicist on one important point—many astrologers, even those who use constellations in their work, are unaware of Ophiuchus' "membership" in the sacred twelve due to the fact that his feet touch the ecliptic. But he is no "thirteenth sign"—he is part and parcel of the span of the Scorpion, and should be recognized, included and honored as such. The Scorpion was seen as a death-dealing creature,[8] and Ophiuchus as a healer—thus combined they represent life-or-death issues and choices.

Nonetheless, if Dr. Tyson is going to attack astrology (one of his very favorite pastimes), a discipline studied and employed by Hipparchus, Ptolemy, Galileo and Kepler, to name a few, it is incumbent upon him, laden with honors and academic credentials as he is, to get it right!

Endnotes

[1]Celestial longitude: the distance between the first point of the tropical zodiac (0 Aries) and any celestial body, measured eastward (to the left on map) along ecliptic. The celestial longitudes of stars are determined by projecting their positions perpendicularly onto the ecliptic.

[2]Constellation boundaries were set by the IAU in 1928, after reports from committees set up for that purpose.

[3]Other distortions forced upon the constellation figures by the IAU include the diminution of the Great Square of Pegasus—"officially" a square no more—it has lost its northeast corner to Andromeda (the fact is, of course, that Alpheratz (aka Sirrah) is, and always has been, both Delta Pegasi, the Navel of Pegasus and Alpha Andromedae, the Head of Andromeda. Another example if IAU meddling is that of the right foot of Auriga the Charioteer (Gamma Aurigae) and the north horn-tip of Taurus (El Nath, Beta Tauri). They are the same star—but "official" sky maps will only own to its being Beta Tauri.

[4]All positions in this article are epoch 2000.0.

[5]To the Greeks Ophiuchus was Aesculapius, God of Medicine.

[6]Our tropical zodiac sign of Taurus was originally the sky figure of the Bull; but now, each year, as the Sun moves through the sign of tropical Taurus it is actually traveling through a skyscape of the stars of the Ram; and tropicalists who call themselves "Aries" were actually born when the Sun traversed the original Pisces Fishes. In just this way, each tropical sign now largely overlays the star figure (or morpheme) that originally came before it. Just as tropical Taureans have backed up onto the Ram, tropical Aries dive with the Fishes; tropical Pisceans swim over most of

the original figure of the Water-Pourer; tropical Aquarians now brave the stormy waves with the Sea-Goat (one arm of the ancient Water-Pourer stretches over him), tropical Capricorns ride the back of the half-human, half-equine Archer, tropical Sagittarians attempt to tame the menacing Scorpion, tropical Scorpios nest in the Scales of Justice (which were, even very far back, both Scales and the great Scorpion's extended claws); tropical Librans now find their balance in the midst of the magnificent Virgin-goddess, (feeling right at home, for she was called "Justicia"), tropical Virgoans have taken over the body and tail of the Lion (but still, at the end of the sign, still possess the upper part of the Virgin's face and head); tropical Leos, while still hanging on to the head and forepaws of the original Lion, have the earlier two-thirds of their sign in the cautious, self-protective Crab; tropical Cancers now envelop the adventurous Twin brothers, tropical Geminis have bravely taken over the thundering, sensual Bull of Heaven, and we are back to where the zodiac started: the Bull, leader of the great cycle of signs from about 4,500 BCE until about 2,300 BCE.

[7]See the Uranometria 2000 grid; it shows that the northwest corner of Cetus definitely lies below the ecliptic.

[8]Royal-and-war star Antares, Alpha Scorpii, lies just under Ophiuchus' intruding left foot; since ancient times it has been known to threaten assassination: it culminates on the charts of Julius Caesar and Abraham Lincoln (who also had Neptune at the star), was the Saturn of Pompey the Great and Cicero, and the Uranus-N Node conjunction of Lord Louis Mountbatten, all of whom were assassinated. The Moon and Asc were aligned with Antares when Lincoln was shot, Mercury when John F. Kennedy was shot, Neptune at two attempts on Gerald Ford's life in 1975, Uranus when Indira Gandhi was assassinated in 1984, and Mars when Yitzhak Rabin was assassinated in 1995. But, of course, all this is sheer coincidence, or so Neil deGrasse Tyson would have us believe.

Bibliography

Allen, Richard Hinckley. *Star Names, their Lore and Meaning.* Dover Publications, Inc., NY, 1963.

Hirshfeld, Alan and Sinnott, Roger W., eds. *Sky Catalogue 2000.0*, 2 vols. Sky Publishing Corp, Cambridge, MA, 1982.

Rosenberg, Diana K. *Secrets of the Ancient Skies, Fixed Stars and Constellations in Natal and Mundane Astrology* (in preparation). Constellation

illustrations are by the author.
Tirion, Wil, Rappapport, Barry, and Lovi, George. *Uranometria 2000.0.* Willmann-Bell, Inc., Richmond, VA,1987-88.
Transactions of the International Astronomers Union, Vol. 4. Cambridge University Press, 1933.
Tyson, Neil deGrasse. *Universe Down to Earth.* Columbia University Press, 1994.

The Enigmatic Love Song of Astronomer Mike Brown

By Edward Snow

"Please don't tell any of my fellow astronomers, but I love astrologers. Really I do," astronomer Mike Brown once declared in his quasi weekly column, *Mike Brown's Planets*. But he swiftly raced to reassure readers that his romance with astrologers was purely platonic.

"Don't get me wrong. I have absolutely no belief whatsoever in the proposition that the positions of planets or stars or moons or anything else that is moving across the sky has or ever had any sort of control over your life, your actions, or your choices. Zero. Really," he claimed.

It's fair to question whether the astronomer's adamant disclaimer suggests he's in denial or maybe looking to cover his backside with skeptical astronomical community pals. In fact, the conundrum appears to be more complex or complicated than that. Really.

Mike Brown's love song warbles on: "If I don't believe in what I must assume would have to be considered a central precept of astrology, how can I possibly claim to love the practitioners?" he asks. Parodying one of the most famous love poems in English literature (Elizabeth Barrett Browning's *How do I Love Thee?)* he succinctly answers his own question: "Let me count the ways."

"Astrologers care about the sky and the positions of the stars and the moon. I care about the sky and the position of the stars and the moon. Astrologers try to understand patterns in the orbits and motions of the planets and determine their meaning. I try to understand patterns in the orbits and motions of the planets and determine their meaning. In a broad general sense we do many of the same things; it's just that our methods are different," he explains.

An Impressive Career

Brown is the California Institute of Technology (Caltech) wunderkind who used the modest equipment at Palomar Observatory near San Diego, Calif., to go on a planet hunting tear in the far reaches of the solar system. As a Wall Street Journal reporter put it, his discoveries "provoked chaos within astronomy circles, calling into question the very meaning of the word planet."

In his best-selling memoir, *How I Killed Pluto and Why It Had It Coming,* the astronomer described the events that culminated in Pluto being kicked-out of the planetary system's inner circle and added to the growing family of so-called dwarf planets, most of which orbit the sun at distances well beyond the orbit of Neptune. On this list are Eris, Haumea, Makemake, Quaoar, Vanuna, Ixon, Sedna and the nameless orphan known only (at this writing) as TNO 2002 TC 302.

And this, we're told, may only be the tip of the iceberg.

In 2006, Brown was named one of Time Magazine's 100 Most Influential People. He has written more than 100 scientific papers and was awarded the Urey Prize for the best young planetary scientist by the American Astronomical Society's Division of Planetary Sciences. He also received the Richard P. Feynman Award for Outstanding Teaching and appears to be on a professional quest to either teach his peers better manners or assuage their fears. Maybe both.

A Curious Love Affair

In the column he titled *I Love Astrologers,* Brown makes the point that astrology and astronomy are brothers "with roots deeper than just the first five letters. Until perhaps the Enlightenment the brothers were inseparable. Copernicus, who made one of the greatest conceptual leaps in human history, pulling the earth out of the center of the universe and replacing it with the sun, was a dedicated astrologer, calculating astrological charts with as much fervor and trying to understand the paths of the planets."

Brown says it's not hard to understand why Copernicus would feel that some connection should be there. "I don't think anyone can watch the movements of the planets and sun and moon and not somehow get a gut feeling that there is somehow meaning in all of that beauty, precision and symmetry."

He continues:

"From their common upbringing, the brothers split in adulthood. They each retained their common interest in the sky, but with thoroughly different ways of looking at it. Astronomy moved to the purely objective realm of descriptive and predictive reality. It moved to science. And a wondrous science it is."

"I can go outside tonight and look up to see the bright glowing star Betelgeuse, the red orb in the upper corner of constellation Orion, and I can tell you a pretty good version of the entire story of its birth in a cloud of gas and dust, its long existence as a smaller and cooler star with hydrogen atoms fusing together in the deep interior, and its recent expansion to form a ball of gas the size of the orbit of Mars," Brown says, adding:

"That we've been able to determine this story at all, simply from looking at the feeble light from these little points in the sky, is as improbable as it is incredible. When I see Betelgeuse at night and stop to think these thoughts I am left in awe."

So what can astrology offer that even comes close to matching? Apparently nothing that might change the astronomer's mind. But this doesn't mean astrology is worthless or potentially dangerous as some would have us believe, he says.

"Astrology is the brother who kept the fascination with the sky, but rather than growing an interest in science kept its interest in humanity. Scientific astronomy, for all its awe-inspiring, mind-expanding and just simply amazing discoveries leaves people and their consciousness out of the picture.

"Astronomy involves people looking up at the heavens, but the heavens are never looking back. Astrology, in contrast, never removed that connection between the sky and the people."

Simplistic Thinking

Brown says he can see no reason why a ball of rock and ice so far from the earth would affect all humanity. And he questions the efficacy of reading psychological meanings into the mythological names astronomers arbitrarily give to newly discovered celestial bodies.

But astronomy and astrology are brothers, he insists.

"Brothers don't always do the same things or make the same choices. But when they maintain their initial ties to where they came from, their connection cannot help but stay strong. What is not to love?" he asks.

Astrologers aren't accustomed to having their discipline so passionately defended by learned men of science. More often, the expectation is that more loquacious members of the astronomical community will proffer their usual churlish comments that ignore the past and disparage a group they know little about. In contrast, Brown is a decent, fair-minded scientist who, in the past, has been willing to share information about his work with astrologers.

"The astrologers who occasionally correspond with me love to hear about new solar system discoveries, figure out orbital relationships and patterns, and speculate about what else might be out there and how everything fits together," he points out.

Researching Distant Sedna

In an article that published in *The Mountain Astrologer* magazine, astrologer Barbara Schermer described her newest research project. Brown, she says, politely answered some of her technical questions and also provided accurate birth data (time, date and place) for himself and for the exact moment when he and colleagues discovered Sedna, the most distant dwarf planet known to be orbiting the sun in our solar system some 8 billion miles from earth. The exact time of discovery is not all that important to astronomers unless an argument over bragging rights erupts. But precise timing provides important clues for astrologers, Schermer says.

The honor of naming a new planetary body is traditionally given to those who discover it. Although Brown and colleagues admittedly find it hard to believe that distant planetoids can influence real events on earth in any way, they nevertheless embraced the tradition of naming celestial bodies for mythological entities—because this practice gives the celestial object "a story."

"Our newly discovered object is the coldest, most distant place known in the solar system, so we feel it is appropriate to name it in honor of Sedna, the Inuit goddess of the sea, who is thought to live at the bottom of the frigid arctic ocean," Brown explained at the time his discovery was submitted to the International Astronomical Union.

According to Schermer, most astrologers would agree (and astronomers would not!) that when naming an object astronomers "are participating in an event of archetypal manifestation that introduces new gods upon the stage of human drama." While it's extremely difficult for scientists to get cozy with such a magical worldview, it's equally hard for astrologers to cave on the fundamental idea that, as Brown so colorfully puts it, the heavens are in fact "looking back."

The Next Paradigm Shift

The dichotomous nature of these positions isn't likely to change for awhile. In the meantime, while we await the next paradigm shift, Brown's thoughtful and congenial dialog is both constructive and helpful while exhibiting rare leadership qualities.

Schermer would argue there's ample observable evidence supporting the astrology side. "As planetary entities are named and their stories located in myth, astrologers pick up on the narrative. Astrological ephemerides are generated and published and astrologers begin to unpack the meanings of the symbols generated and study the many stories created by the myth.

"Astrologers may empirically research the planet's transits through their own lives or observe cultural and historic events in apparent synchrony with the planet's positions. Or we may analyze the charts of individuals who have that planet prominent in their own birth chart," she says.

Schermer believes her research demonstrates that, over the past 140 years,

Sedna has presented a consistent ecological or environmental message. The working hypothesis for her study: "Sedna represents a new and powerful voice calling us to a balanced and sustainable relationship with nature."

In addition to Sedna's discovery chart, Schermer analyzed the birth charts of individuals with a known passion for protecting the environment, such as Jacques Cousteau and Rachel Carson. She also studied the astrological charts of organizations like the Sierra Club, and release dates for films like *Whalerider*. Because he is a member of the Sierra Club, Mike Brown's birth chart was included in the data pool as well.

The astrologer found Sedna prominently placed in each of the charts she analyzed and was able to conclude that the dwarf planet's mission "is to promote interdependence, balance, beauty, transcendence, humility, prosperity, ethical purpose, hope and the resolve to renew the Earth and all its creatures in light of these values."

Although Sedna was only recently discovered, Schermer says the frigid planet "has been speaking for generations through history, traditional wisdom, prophetic declamation, climatic spasm, scientific discovery, spiritual insight and dawning social awareness,"

What if Astrology Is Real?

By Edward Snow

Dr. Joseph "Deepak" Vidmar has done something others phasing through a midlife crisis might contemplate but rarely do. He was a psychology professor at a Louisiana university and the past president of the Louisiana Psychological Association when he reached the decision that propelled him into a serious-minded pursuit of enlightenment in the spiritual calm of India and other Eastern countries.

True, he was fed up with establishment views in America, and chafed at the fact that professional colleagues rarely shared his enthusiasm for astrology. But he once told a BBC journalist the main reason he left his comfortable lifestyle and professional achievements behind was because this existence failed to make him happy.

He gave it all up to become Deepak, an ashram astrologer living in India in sparse and frugal surroundings. He sums up his passion for astrology with these words:

"Astrology is the most misunderstood subject of all human knowledge. It is not about knowing your future…it is about knowing yourself. It is about the journey of your soul through this world and what this is all about. And it is about the process of self-awareness and what is true for you," he observes.

"Astrology can tell you what, when, where, and how. However, something else will have to tell you why," he adds.

Although there are few worldly trappings in the living space he now calls home, Professor Vidmar hardly fits romanticized notions sometimes associated with disaffected societal dropouts. Among his meager possessions are books, papers and the computer that keeps him tethered to the outside world.

From time to time, he drops in to remind anyone who might be listening of the ways intellectual priorities in the western world continue to run amuck.

A Life or Death Issue...

A few years ago, for a major astrological journal, he wrote a scathing critique of the Shawn Carlson research study which, according to the researcher, purportedly proved that astrology doesn't work. More recently, an essay published in the OxfordStudent newspaper synthesized his adamant views on how western science is dodging obvious astrological truths.

Dr. Vidmar's OxfordStudent essay is published here in its entirety. He writes:

"What if astrology is real? It is not only a multi-trillion dollar question; it is a life or death issue. It is the missing element in all the fumbling disciplines of quasi-knowledge being taught in the universities today. Without this missing element, not only can the institutions not solve the current problems we are facing, they are actually creating them.

"Let's be clear about what we are talking about. We are not talking about a mystic teller with broken teeth and dirty fingernails who will tell you your fortune. We are talking about a universal constant that shows its effects in every body of knowledge we possess today.

"Astrology is just a word made up from Greek roots in the 14th Century. It is many thousands of years older than that and has had many names and applications. It is better in this age to call it the ET Effect.

"As a licensed psychologist and professor of psychology for 20 years, I gave over 3,000 psychological evaluations. As an ashram astrologer in India for 20 years I have given over 3,000 sessions. The end conclusion is that the ET Effect in the field of personality is real.

"If the ET Effect is real in the field of personality, then it may be a real effect in other disciplines also. I have just spent 50 hour weeks for the past five years researching this question. The end conclusion is that the effect is universal.

"Take biology. We are not disconnected and isolated on Earth from the rest of the Universe. F.A. Brown is the classic researcher here and has found fiddler crabs, clams, potatoes, seaweed, etc. to be phase locked to cosmic frequencies of solar and lunar cycles. The whole phenomenon of exogenous biological clocks pertains but is unexplained.

"Chemistry also—Giorgio Piccardi has extensively tested that chemical reactions on Earth vary according to sunspot cycles. Maki Takata found flocculation of albumen in blood serum varied to sunspots and sunrise. A.M. Comunetti found electrical conductivity of pure water changed with cosmic factors.

"And even in history, the orthodox position of a linear progressive model is illusionary and not supported by the evidence. Instead, the flow of events is cyclical with ups and downs.

"Whilst I have mentioned just these fields, similar situations apply in economics, physics and medicine.

"If these results were in any other field but 'astrology' the evidence would have lead to more funding than the LHC (the Large Hadron Collider). This is a culture bound prejudice since 1666 when science/society went psychotic thinking reductionism/facts (left brain) could explain anything, while pattern recognition (right brain) was ignored."

Putting Some Important Astrological History in Perspective

By Edward Snow

Your computer's spell checker may not know how to correctly spell his name, but medieval astrologer/astronomer Johannes Kepler is no stranger to those who study the night sky from entirely different—and disparate—perspectives.

Kepler was the brilliant 17th century astrologer who discovered the three laws of planetary motion named for him. Though the idea must have seemed wildly counterintuitive to contemporaries, Kepler was able to mathematically prove the earth and neighboring planets all were orbiting the sun in predictable elliptical orbits—as Copernicus before him had suggested.

Astrological researcher David Cochrane describes Kepler as one of the greatest scientists of all time. What Kepler was able to achieve "marked an important transition to a scientific age where mathematics combines with careful observations to explain the rational basis for a great many things," he said.

Kepler's Accomplishments

But lost on many modern observers is the fact that Kepler's accomplishments also marked a crowning triumph for astrology and ongoing efforts by serious astrologers to pragmatically improve their craft by producing more accurate birth charts (horoscopes).

Historian John North makes the point that had Kepler not been an astrologer he would very probably have failed to produce his planetary astronomy in the form we have it today.

What bothers Cochrane is revisionist history that trivializes Kepler's motives.

For example, he says an article about Kepler posted on the prestigious Harvard.edu website derisively portrays the mathematical genius as someone who, driven by economic necessity, was reduced "to making astrological predictions for noblemen who wanted their fortunes told."

Kepler did earn a living reading horoscopes for the rich and powerful. But, Cochrane says, those who say Kepler only practiced astrology to survive have not examined the evidence very carefully.

Because his contribution to astronomy was so profound, Kepler is often romantically identified with the scientific revolution that purportedly rescued humanity from the slagheap of medieval mysticism. But this, Cochrane insists, was never his intention.

"Kepler fully believed in and endorsed astrology as a meaningful and important study. Those who trivialize his sincere involvement distort the historical record," he believes.

Produced Yearly Almanacs

Other modern astrologers have weighed in on the subject. Robert Currey writes that Kepler produced yearly almanacs with astrological and other phenomena. In addition to the three laws of planetary motion he also connected the tidal cycle with the lunar nodes.

In 1601, Kepler wrote *De Fundamentis Astrologiae Cetoribus*, a book defending the physical foundations of astrology. In it he revealed his rapture with the Pythagorean concept of celestial harmony and what he called the "geometricizing" God in creation.

Currey says Kepler drew inspiration from classical Greek thinkers but also was a devoutly religious man who described himself to mentor Michael Maestlin as a "Lutheran astrologer." In line with the changing times he wanted a reformation of astrology, but implored theologians, physicians and philosophers not to "throw the baby out with the bath water."

In 1606 Kepler wrote to Oxford scientist Thomas Harriot, informing the academic that 10 years earlier he had rejected the division of the Zodiac into 12 astrological signs and other traditional astrological concepts. At the time he told Harriot he was focused solely on aspects (the angular relationships of planets to each other expressed in degrees) and was transferring astrology to the science of harmonics.

"On the surface of it, these widely quoted comments seem to support the popular myth that Kepler did not believe in astrology but had to practice it simply to pay the bills. But the comments do not appear to be a genuine reflection of Kepler's personal view of astrology," Currey writes, adding:

"Kepler was seeking information from Harriot on his experiments in refraction. Clearly he was attempting to recast astrology within what he thought might be a more acceptable Harmonic-Pythagorean framework."

Although Kepler apparently worried about his professional image he continued to publish his almanacs until 1624. However, in correspondence with Maestlin, he did express his concern that the almanacs might harm his scientific reputation, Currey points out.

In 1999, an astronomer found a horoscope drawn up by Kepler for an Austrian nobleman. The horoscope clearly showed the traditional positions of the houses and astrological signs, which Kepler told Harriot in 1606 he had stopped using 10 years earlier.

"The Austrian nobleman was born in 1587. For Kepler's claim to Harriot to be true, the Austrian would have been less than 10 years old—and Kepler age 25—when the chart was made," Currey said.

In two private letters to Maestlin in 1611 Kepler discussed the horoscopes of his family and the astrological reasons for his son's death. This private exchange, where no financial gain was involved, reveals Kepler's interest in astrology "was unquestionably sincere," he added.

Psychological Insights Redefining Astrology

By Glenn Perry, PhD

AstroPsychology is a reformulation of astrology in terms of psychological concepts and practices. A core tenet of Astro-Psychology is that planets symbolize functions that are oriented toward satisfying the needs of the signs they rule. In astrology, every planet is said to rule a particular sign, which simply means that certain planets and signs have an affinity for each other. Because the planet is the more active principle, its responsibility is to fulfill the needs symbolized by the sign it rules. Signs are motives; planets are their active agents.

Another way of saying this is that a planet symbolizes a psychological faculty, which can be defined as an inherent power or ability to perform functions. Planetary functions are the normal, proper or characteristic actions of that planet; thus, for example, Mars symbolizes the functions of asserting, starting and competing, which are in the service of Aries' needs for freedom, adventure and survival. While early humans experienced planetary archetypes as messages from gods originating outside of their own minds, today we recognize archetypes as the core feelings, needs, and values that constitute our inner life.

Again, planetary functions are motivated by the need(s) of the sign that planet rules. This implies that motivation and function are as inseparable as a rocket and its fuel tank. Each sign-planet pairing can be regarded as a system. When we talk about the body, we refer to specific systems such as the cardiovascular system, the gastrointestinal system, and the endocrine system. Likewise, there are psychological systems. Aries-Mars rules the competitive/assertion system, Taurus-Venus the security/stability system, and Capricorn-Saturn the control/mastery system. A sign-planet is a motivational system because it entails an interaction between two components of the psyche: sign and planet. As needs, signs motivate their ruling planets to perform specific functions, and these functions involve appropriate actions that serve the underlying motive.

Maslow's Insights

Abraham Maslow (1968) proposed that human beings are born with an essential nature that is analogous with physical structure. Just so in astrology, psychological functions are analogous to their biological corollaries. The functions of digestion and elimination, for example, are paralleled by corresponding psychological processes ruled by Virgo-Mercury and Scorpio-Pluto. Just as we digest food, so we digest information, breaking it down into useful parts and assimilating it into our cognitive structure. This is the function of Virgo-Mercury.

We also eliminate on a psychological level, as when we experience catharsis, abreaction, or overcome a destructive mental habit—all of which are ruled by the Scorpio-Pluto system. This is why biological and corollary psychological functions are ruled by the same sign-planet system.

Whereas the Virgo-Mercury system governs the intestines, gastrointestinal system, and overall food metabolism, it also governs psychological process of analyzing and utilizing information in the service of competence. In other words, Virgo is about the metabolizing of information—a clear corollary to the process of digestion on a biological level. Likewise, biological and psychological processes of elimination are ruled by Scorpio-Pluto.

On a biological level, Scorpio-Pluto governs the sexual/generative organs, which include the bladder, prostate gland, testicles, colon, and rectum. Note that these organ systems are involved in processes of ejection and elimination; ovulation and menstruation in the female and ejaculation in the male. Psychologically, Scorpio-Pluto rules sexuality and tends to be penetrating, erotic, and regenerative by its very nature. It also involves psycho-eliminative processes such as the purging of destructive emotions and habits. These two examples—Virgo-Mercury and Scorpio-Pluto—should suffice to illustrate how a sign-planet system is analogous to a biological organ, and symbolizes a specific type of action that is in the service of a psychological need, or motive.

Just as the need of a sign can be inferred from behaviors that characterize that sign, so a planet's functions can be inferred from actions that characterize its nature. This is simply a matter of inductive reasoning. By observing characteristic actions of a planet, one can discern where the actions are leading to—in short, the purpose of the behavior. An action is any behavior that is goal-directed, or done for a reason. If one observes that Neptune is implicated in spiritual strivings, compassion for suffering, redemptive love, charity, psi abilities, fantasy, and dreams, then the functions of Neptune would account for actions classified as Neptunian.

If we call Neptune the *Transcendent Faculty,* this may suffice, for spiritual strivings are in the service of transcending the separate self-sense and uniting with a higher consciousness. Concern for the less fortunate, charity, and redemptive love require one to transcend self-interest and act to relieve the suffering of others. Psi abilities involve cognitive capacities that transcend rational intellect and sensory experience, while fantasy and dreams involve the perception of ideals and possibilities that transcend everyday, material reality. While no single word does justice to the diverse forms this archetypal process takes, *Transcendent Faculty* is as good a term as any. It may be that the best name for a planetary faculty is simply the planet itself—in this case, the faculty of *Neptune.*

Any characteristic action of a planet can be converted from a verb into a noun, which gives us a name for that function. Recall that planetary functions are the normal, proper, or characteristic actions of that planet. For example, Neptune symbolizes the verbs to imagine, to empathize, and to intuit. By converting these verbs into nouns we get three functions of Neptune: imagination, empathy, and intuition. Each term captures one facet of a complex, psychological faculty. Of course, there are other functions of Neptune beyond these three.

Again, functions are always in the service of needs. For every need represented by a sign, there is a planetary function devoted to the fulfillment of that need. Signs and planets form verb-noun pairs, as it were, the planet being the active agent (verb) of the sign-need (noun) over which it rules. Saturn, for instance, is the planet that rules Capricorn. The need of Capricorn can be described as the drive for perfection in material form—or, put simply, the need for order, structure and control. Saturn, as the verb form and active agent of Capricorn, fulfills its needs by ordering, structuring, and controlling within the behavioral environment. Hence, Saturn represents the functions of order, structure, and control. In this regard, every planet symbolizes a particular kind of activity. Planets are actors and each one acts in a different way.

In an actual chart, Saturn would be in a particular sign. When a planet occupies a sign, the sign operates as an adverb qualifying the planetary verb. Let us say that Saturn is in Gemini. Thus, we have the syntax of an astrological sentence: the need of Capricorn (noun) is fulfilled by Saturn (verb) in a Gemini manner (adverb). In short, the need for order is fulfilled by achieving intellectually. Saturn in Gemini represents the drive for perfection through the ordering of mental constructs. If Saturn is highlighted in the natal chart (e.g., conjunct the Sun), we might have an individual, for instance, with an obsessive need to structure language into a logical system. Perhaps he might write a book on linguistics or devise a theory of syntax. The Gemini sign placement merely suggests how Saturn fulfills its Capricorn-need and what some possible outcomes might be.

The point here is that needs symbolized by signs provide the motivation that triggers functions represented by planets. How and whether those functions satisfy their motivating needs is indicated by a host of additional factors including the planet's sign and house position and its aspects to other planets. The degree to which a planet can satisfy its sign-need is a measure of that planet's functionality (or *dys*functionality). This is a topic of considerable complexity, however. Interested readers might explore the books below for more information.

References

Maslow, A. (1968). *Toward a Psychology of Being*. Princeton, NJ: Van Nostrand.

Perry, G. (2012). *An Introduction to AstroPsychology*. Haddam Neck, CT: AAP Press.

Perry, G. (2012). *Depth Analysis of the Natal Chart*. Haddam Neck, CT: AAP Press.

How Integral Astrology Connects The Dots…

By Edward Snow

What do transpersonal psychology, chaos and complexity theories, general evolution theory and the human potential movement have to do with astrology?

In his latest book, *Integral Astrology, Understanding the Ancient Discipline in the Contemporary World,* astrologer, author and educator Armand Diaz, PhD, describes how astrology connects with a new paradigm that is emerging in Western civilization.

"Leading developmental researchers are extending psychology upwards, linking it with mystical states to embrace spirituality. Coordinating fields of information both old and new, integral theorists are creating a truly holistic approach to the many ways of knowing that are part of the human experience," he says.

Diaz is a consciousness researcher and professional counseling astrologer with a bachelor's degree in psychology from Columbia University, a master's degree from Hofstra University and a doctorate from the California Institute of Integral Studies (CIIS) in San Francisco, where he won an Esalen scholarship for his study on the lives of psychic mediums. Currently, he is an adjunct assistant professor at Hofstra and Brooklyn College and is articles editor for the Astrology News Service (ANS).

In addition to astrology, he says his interests are in the areas of Jungian psychology, the astrology of healing and the healing power of non-ordinary states of consciousness. He studied divination and oracles for many years, primarily working with Tarot and the I Ching.

In an interview with the Astrology News Service (ANS), Diaz provided these insights:

ANS: What is divination and to what good purpose is it applied in an astrological reading?

Diaz: To *divine* literally means to contact the mind of the god(s)—although I think most practitioners today have a slightly less grand view of what they are doing! Divination includes astrology, tarot and a myriad of other means and devices for accessing information that isn't available through the senses or our other usual approaches to life—such as thinking and logic, feeling, and so on. Astrology is a means of divination because it's a way of interfacing the physical world and the underlying symbolic patterns that inform the cosmos. Even among systems of divination, as well as psychic and mediumistic phenomena, astrology is unique because it assumes a correspondence between the two at all levels, including everyday reality.

I think the greatest value of any form of divination is that it offers perspective for most people most of the time. It isn't about what is going to happen. It's about understanding the patterns involved and the kinds of choices that are open to us. It's a little like a weather forecast—meteorologists tell you if it's going to be sunny or rain. But they don't tell you if you are going to be dry or wet because they assume you'll take the information they are giving you and make an informed choice.

One of the things I discovered when working with psychic-mediums is that they don't view what they do as extraordinary, and they have no desire to impress anyone with their skills. They see themselves as helping professionals. I think most astrologers have the same approach. Like those in most helping professions, astrologers can help people to get a different perspective on issues they have.

ANS: How do academic peers reconcile your interests in Tarot and the I Ching?

Diaz: And astrology! A few express some interest. Most are bemused, but many of those eventually agree that there may be some validity to non-material phenomena. It's about the same with my students, by the way.

ANS: What are the most important things going on in the field of consciousness research and what have these to do with astrology?

Diaz: Consciousness research has, in my opinion, already successfully demonstrated that information and even conscious awareness can exist and be transited apart from physical means. Now the big question is: what is happening? A number of people, including biologist Rupert Sheldrake, are attempting to answer that question, developing working models and theories. Many of these are testable and successfully meet scientific criteria.

For astrology, the question is whether we can be included in this, and if so, how. Over the last 50 years or so, there has been a significant and serious challenge to the view that the material world is the only "real" world. A new paradigm is emerging in which consciousness is seen as an integral part of existence. Astrology and this new paradigm have followed a parallel course of development, although they have done so at considerable distance from each other.

The problem is, much of consciousness research is focused on finding out if specific information can be shared across space and time. On the other hand, astrology—as it is practiced by most Western astrologers—is symbolic in nature, and symbols are hard to measure. It's like the difference between measuring how many words are in Richard III and measuring what the play means.

ANS: What is integral astrology?

Diaz: Integral means *whole*, and an integral approach to astrology is one that recognizes not only astrology but a variety of non-astrological factors, as well. Although astrology provides extraordinarily helpful information, making optimal use of it is dependent on understanding all kinds of things, such as a person's culture, gender, and education.

Key to integral astrology is the understanding that how astrological symbols manifest—as events in people's lives or as interior experiences, for example—is related to an individual's degree of conscious awareness, and that's something you can't know from looking at a birth chart. Sometimes the emphasis is on how specific events will unfold, sometimes it's about understanding the options that are available, sometimes it's about how a person is feeling, or about the meaning of a particular time in one's life. Matching the client to the right astrologer, who is practicing the right astrology for the situation, is very important.

As with many disciplines—psychology, for example—there are many different schools of astrology, each using its own techniques and each having areas of life where it will have greater and lesser value. Integral astrology provides a way of recognizing the value of all of these schools, and organizing them in a cohesive way. So the integral approach to astrology isn't about a set of new techniques, it's about knowing how to best apply the tools that we have.

ANS: What lessons can we learn from ancient astrologers?

Diaz: Well, for one thing, ancient astrologers actually looked at the sky, and taking a peak up there every now and then is a good idea for us, too. A contemporary astrologer could easily work from an underground location, never seeing the stars and planets. In a sense, that's appropriate, as astrology has become more abstract and formalized over the centuries. But I feel there's great value in connecting with the sky when you can, and remembering why it is that we began to see meaning threaded through the cosmos at every level.

ANS: What can people do to live out the best expression of the energies they're born with?

Diaz: Astrology describes the basic, fundamental energetic patterns that inform our approach to life. But astrology says absolutely nothing about our degree of awareness, how conscious we are, or in other words, our level of psycho spiritual development. Astrology tells us what we have packed in our bags for our evolutionary journey, but not how much progress we have made along the way.

That's why people born at the same time—like twins—can often be so very different. It also helps to explain why some people seem to be tossed around by fate, while others have a greater degree of control. So the key to living out the best expression of our energies is to bring as much awareness and compassion to them as possible.

Part II

The Evidence...

Sleep Researcher Delivers for Astrology

By Edward Snow

A reluctant college professor who feared his discovery might cause peers to regard him as a "lunatic" inadvertently stumbled onto an important research finding that flies in the face of conventional scientific explanations for the way people experience reality on planet earth.

Curiously, all of the test subjects in Professor Christian Cajochen's laboratory at the University of Basel in Switzerland were asleep when study data was collected—some more soundly than others.

London Times science correspondent Tom Whipple provides this account:

Prof. Cajochen, a psychiatrist who studies circadian rhythms, was having cocktails with colleagues at a local pub. The full moon had risen and was flooding their table with light.

When the conversation turned to shop talk some of the professor's colleagues complained they slept less well when the moon was full. After years of studying sleep patterns, Prof. Cajochen realized he had enough data to check out these claims and made a decision to do so the next day.

It was the researcher's intention to prove his friends wrong by disproving their hypothesis: sleep patterns are influenced by the full moon. "To my surprise I couldn't," he reportedly said.

What the psychiatrist found was a result he knew conventional scientists would be inclined to heckle. Most scientists believe they have the physical universe pretty well figured out and moon beams don't figure in their calculations.

Also, almost certainly, Prof. Cajochen must have realized that his findings would provide aid and comfort for astrologers and support for the ancient cosmological world view that embraces organic connectedness between the heavens and earth.

For his test, Prof. Cajochen used data collected 10 years earlier for another study. Only this time, 33 participants between the ages of 12 and 75 were grouped based on whether the moon was new or full when they entered the laboratory for extended testing.

Not So Surprising Results

Results of the test are described in the journal *Current Biology.* The researchers found that those who came into the sleep laboratory during a full moon took five minutes longer to fall asleep and had 20 minutes less sleep on average. Even more significantly, test subjects spent 30 percent less time in restful deep sleep than those who entered the lab under a different lunar phase.

"It was a quite considerable effect," Prof. Cajochen told the *London Times.*

But it took him more than four years to publish the results because he worried what peers in the scientific community might think.

One expert who might sympathize with the researcher's reticence to tell his story is biologist and author Rupert Sheldrake. His newest book, *Science Set Free,* presents the idea that science is being held back by centuries-old assumptions that have hardened into dogma.

"The biggest scientific delusion of all is that science already knows the answers. The details still need working out but, in principle, the fundamental questions are settled," he said.

British astrologer, writer and lecturer Robert Currey commented on the study's credibility. What adds weight to Cajochen's study is the fact that data used by the research team was collected 10 years earlier for a different study, he says.

"By being retrospective, critics will find it hard to claim any experimental or selection bias of subjects or data. A simple mechanism such as increased moonlight can also be ruled out as the subjects slept in a dark room in the sleep laboratory," he added.

The full Moon is a major aspect or angle astrologers call an opposition. From our vantage point on earth, this angle or aspect occurs when the Sun and Moon—or other planetary bodies—line up 180 degrees apart in opposing astrological signs,

Among other things, the full Moon opposition may coincide with a period of increased stress or tension. The individual's vitality (represented by the sun) and personal or emotional needs (the moon) may be conflicted in some way, Currey says.

"Perhaps the urge to be active and creative takes away from satisfying bodily needs like sleep. Conceivably, this lack of sleep might even account for the unusual behavior that tends to occur around the full moon according to lunar lore," he noted.

British astrologer and Editor Pat Harris, PhD, says spiritually-attuned Tibetan monks would probably agree with this assessment, at least in part.

Monks Attuned to Moon

Harris is editor of *Correlation*, a journal published by the Astrological Association of Great Britain (AA). She says the monks are very much attuned to the moon's phases, using them to regulate sleep patterns among other things.

"The scientific experiment at the University of Basel seems to confirm the monks' experiences" she says.

"It could be argued that the monks have conscious expectations regarding how the lunar phase will affect their behavior. However, this confounding factor doesn't apply to the Switzerland sleep study.

"From secondary reports and the researcher's summary we learn that neither the 33 volunteers nor the scientists conducting the tests were aware of the lunar phase at any time," she said.

Famous Test of Astrology Seriously Flawed

By Edward Snow

Results of a research study that skeptics have used for more than three decades to debunk and deride astrology "violated the demands of fairness and common norms of statistical analysis," according to an article published in the *Journal of Scientific Exploration*.

What's more, in his critique, author Suitbert Ertel of the GEM Institute of Psychology in Gottingen, Germany, argues that the study organized by researcher Shawn Carlson and known as "A Double Blind Study of Astrology" followed a faulty, piecemeal analytical approach to the wrong conclusions.

A statistical expert, Ertel is a professor emeritus at Gottingen University and the author of numerous research articles. *The Tenacious Mars Effect*, a book he co-authored with American Kenneth Irving, defended the statistical credibility of astrological effects reported by French statistician Michel Gauquelin.

The Carlson study is widely viewed by skeptic groups as the test that successfully demonstrated the inability of professional astrologers to correctly match individual birth charts with personality profiles generated by a standard psychological personality test. The three-part study also has been cited as evidence that individuals don't appear to know themselves all that well, and can't distinguish between their own and other birth charts (horoscopes) interpreted by professional astrologers.

The controversial study published in the prestigious science journal *Nature* in 1985 and is referred to today by more than 400 Internet pages listed on the Google search engine, which is more than any other research paper of its kind.

Carlson claimed that failed tests involving student volunteers and professional astrologers from the San Francisco Bay Area "produced a strong case against natal astrology as practiced by reputable astrologers." Professor Ertel reanalyzed data from the study and found this claim to be "untenable."

Astrologers participating in the high profile study performed much better than may be generally believed, he observed.

Test Vehicles Described

In one of the three tests conducted by Carlson, professional astrologers were asked to match the birth charts of student volunteers with personality profiles generated by the California Psychological Inventory (CPI) questionnaire. Birth charts were cast for 116 volunteer students, and each volunteer was asked to complete the lengthy CPI questionnaire.

The birth charts of the volunteers were then divided among 28 participating astrologers. For comparison purposes, astrologers were given three CPI personality profiles with every birth chart. One of the profiles was a match for the chart and the other two were two randomly selected profiles matching other volunteers in the pool.

Simply, the idea was to determine if the astrologers would be able to collectively match the charts with the correct CPI profiles in a statistically meaningful way. As part of the assignment, the astrologers were asked to identify which profile was the best, second- and third-best "fit" with the natal chart, and to rank how strongly they felt about their choices on a scale from one to 10.

A similar test was done to see if student test subjects could identify their own CPI personality profiles from a group that included their own and two others. A third test was devised to see if the student volunteers would perform equally well, or badly, when the personality profiles were prepared by professional astrologers.

Effectively, the design for all three tests was the same. But student volunteers were not asked to subjectively rank or indicate how strongly they felt about their choices.

It was Carlson's conclusion that the astrologers failed to match horoscopes with the correct profiles. He also reported that the student volunteers were unable to identify their own CPI profiles, and fared no better when the written profiles were prepared by professional astrologers.

A failed or chance result would mean that subjects only picked the correct profiles about 33 percent of the time (once in every three tries), which is roughly the result Carlson reported for all three tests.

When the study was completed in 1983, Carlson was a PhD candidate in physics at the University of California with no special training or expertise in psychological testing. Concerns about the methods used and conclusions reached quickly surfaced. For example, Carlson was criticized for asking the astrologers to do something the CPI specifically warned against: interpreting scores without any prior experience using the test vehicle in the way it was intended to be used by trained professional psychologists.

Because the CPI results in a different profile for men and women, no psychologist would attempt to interpret the CPI without knowing the gender of the test subjects. However, the astrologers later claimed that Carlson deliberately withheld this information from them. Another concern focused on publication of the research paper in *Nature's* "Commentary" section, the only articles section of the journal that is at the editor's discretion. Content published here is not subjected to the peer review process.

Fairness Issues Raised

Ertel's critical assessment of the study raised fairness issues, questioned the sample size, found flaws with the methodology used, and noted the possibility that careless data handling may have tainted the results. Even more damning, he said the researcher's "piecemeal approach to statistical analysis" contributed to calculation errors.

The tests involving student volunteers were especially suspect. Ertel noted that half of the data ratings were so poor they could not be analyzed, and the half that could be analyzed was not carefully completed. More than one in three students failed to complete their assignments.

The astrologers were more motivated, but Ertel argues that a two-choice format (pair comparison) would have been the more fair way to conduct the tests "because this approach minimizes the complexity of the subject's task while increasing the precision of results."

At the time, astrologers protested that the profiles they were asked to compare were very similar. More fairly, in a test like this, astrologers should be asked to compare the profiles of individuals known to have dissimilar personality traits, Ertel believes.

He points out that Carlson initially intended to see if the astrologers could select the correct profile as either their first or second choice at a statistically higher than expected rate but "ignored his own protocol without giving reasons." Based on his reanalysis of the data, Ertel confirmed that the astrologers were able to select the correct profile as either their first or second choice at a rate significantly better than expected by chance.

With statistical significance, the astrologers also were able to identify which personality profile was the poorest "fit," a finding that also contradicts Carlson's original claim. And a statistical reanalysis of the one to 10 numerical ranking system the astrologers were asked to use to subjectively indicate how strongly they felt about their individual choices weighed in their favor as well.

In view of at least two significant test results, Carlson's claim that we are now in a position to argue a surprisingly strong case against astrology as practiced by reputable astrologers isn't justified, Ertel insists.

Unique Study Links Venus to Romantic Choices

By Edward Snow

Perhaps you've experienced a high-octane romance that began with heightened expectations but inexplicably ended on the scrap heap?

Like Ravel's musical masterpiece Bolero, the romantic cadence may have soared to an exhilarating crescendo. Only in your love song, the orchestra hit some sour notes and the relationship's rhythm was shattered beyond repair.

Astrologer Paul Westran has a tested theory about relationships. In a rigorous, eight year study involving 1,300 couples, he examined the correlations between planetary alignments and real events in people's lives and came up with some surprising results.

Curiously, Westran's research failed to support the popular idea that certain sun signs are more compatible (with each other) than others. But he did find evidence that Venus, the planet astrologers have traditionally identified with the principle of attraction, appears to impact personal relationships in predictable ways.

His research supports the idea that angular alignments between planets, what astrologers call aspects, appear to work the way astrologers say they should. He also found statistical support for the method astrologers call synastry, which compares the angular alignments between planets in compared natal birth charts or horoscopes. Most commonly, this technique is used to evaluate compatibility potential between couples.

Surprisingly, Westran also showed that planets that are progressed or moved ahead using the technique astrologers call "secondary progressions" are significantly more involved at the start-up of relationships than previously suspected.

Why Relationships Wax and Wane

In the study, favorable aspects between the sun and Venus turned up in the compared synastry charts of couples a lot more frequently than expected by chance. This was an important finding for astrology, but Westran had other questions. For example, is there a better astrological explanation for why intensity levels in relationships tend to wax and wane the way they do. Can astrologers more accurately determine not only who might be attracted to whom but how the relationship might progress over time? What role, if any, do progressed planets play in the unfolding drama?

Normally, secondary progressions are used to help time events in individual birth charts. Astrologers calculate how far the sun, moon and planets have progressed around the horoscope wheel using a day-for-a-year formula. For every year that passes, planets in the progressed horoscope are advanced the number of degrees they have actually traveled in a single day, either forward or backwards (if retrograde). To find how far planets have progressed by age 30, the astrologer simply counts forward 30 days from the date of birth and casts a chart for that day.

In a progressed chart, the sun advances about one degree per day, but the progress of the moon and planets is uneven with planets closer to the sun in tighter orbits typically moving around the wheel more swiftly. In this race, Mercury and Venus are usually track stars when compared with foot-dragging Jupiter and Saturn. And the earth-orbiting moon moves with lightning quickness.

Westran believes the major finding emerging from his study is that progressed synastry aspects are powerful indicators of how relationships will

Observed and Expected Sun Venus Synastry and Progressed Synastry Aspects in 1300 Relationships										
n-1300	nSun-nVenus		nSun-pVenus		pSun-nVenus		pSun-pVenus		Total	
2.017° orb	Observed	Expected	Observed	Expected	Observed	Expected	Observed	Expected	Observed	Expected
Trine	73	58.74	80	58.74	75	58.74	74	58.74	302	234.96
Conjunction	42	29.37	40	29.37	35	29.37	44	29.37	161	117.48
Opposition	42	29.37	42	29.37	37	29.37	42	29.37	163	117.48
Square	39	58.74	59	58.74	67	58.74	59	58.74	225	234.96
Sextile	62	58.74	45	58.74	60	58.74	63	58.74	230	234.96
Quincunx	63	58.74	73	58.74	55	58.74	65	58.74	256	234.96
Semisextile	76	58.74	55	58.74	73	58.74	39	58.74	243	234.96

evolve over time. He likens natal synastry to a photograph or a message fixed in time. Progressed synastry aspects are more like a movie with a beginning, middle and definable end.

In a couple's natal synastry chart, Venus may not be forming a major aspect with the sun. But this may no longer be the case 30 years later when the couple meets for the first time. With progressed synastry, aspects can be observed dynamically forming, conjoining and subsequently moving out of orb (outside their range of influence) at the end. In his study, Westran was able to show that progressing synastry aspects dynamically reflect or correspond with romantic developments in the lives of real people.

Sun/Venus Aspects Obvious

From his home in Perth, Australia, Westran runs a successful astrological consultancy with clients on four continents. He is a former crime analyst and forensic software expert and explains that the astrological research activity began as "exploratory analysis." Almost immediately, Sun/Venus aspects stood out and were showing up between progressed horoscopes with great regularity as well.

For the research, Westran needed accurate birth data and confirmable biographical information. The only option was to use public figures and celebrities, which meant relying extensively on well researched products like the AstroDatabank celebrity database. However, each personal history needed to be carefully checked before trying to determine whether the astrology agreed with the couples' personal stories or not. At first, he created research matrices and counted aspects manually but eventually developed software to calculate the aspects. However, for years it was a laborious manual process.

Path of Charles and Diana's progressed Sun progressed Venus trine 1961 to 1996

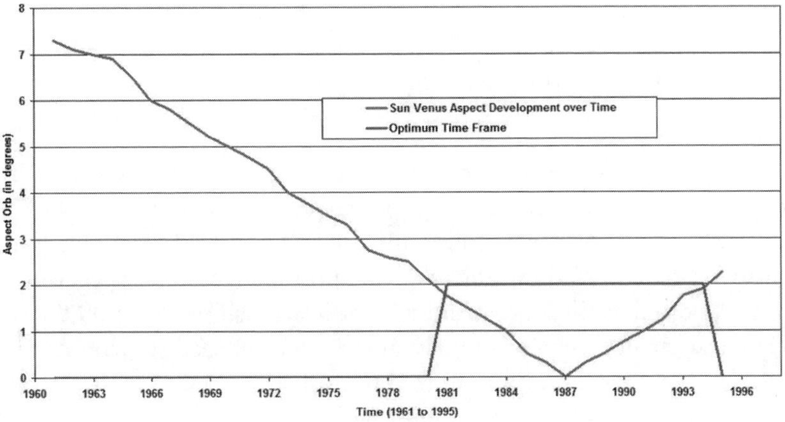

William and Kate progressed Venus natal Venus trine

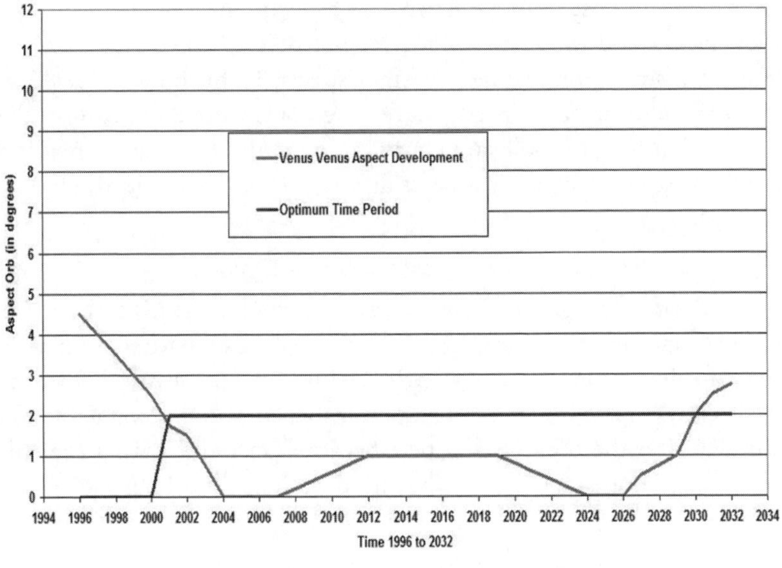

The major aspects astrologers consider are the conjunction, which occurs when celestial bodies are closely aligned in the same sign, and the opposition, which occurs when planets are roughly 180 degrees apart in opposite signs. Also considered are the compatible 120 degree trine, the stressful 90 degree square, and, to a lesser extent, the helpful 60 degree sextile. Among the progressed synastry aspects considered in Westran's study were natal Sun and natal Venus, natal Sun and progressed Venus, progressed Sun and natal Venus, and progressed Sun and progressed Venus.

Convincingly, the study confirmed that Sun/Venus synastry aspects, both natal and progressed, turned up more frequently than expected at the start of relationships. When taking into account all of the possible Sun/Venus synastry connections, the odds that positive synastry aspects would turn up as often as they did at the start of relationships were 900,000 to one against chance, or substantially greater than needed to demonstrate statistical significance. Although less impressively, certain synastry alignments of Venus with Venus and Venus with Mars presented at the start of relationships with statistical significance as well.

Based on a careful evaluation of every natal and progressed synastry chart collected, Westran is convinced that progressed synastry aspects are more powerful and intense than natal synastry aspects. In arriving at this conclusion he was aided by the unique format he created to graphically illustrate and track progressing synastry aspects. In his book, *When Stars Collide*, the author presents page after page of documented case studies and uses what he calls "collision charts" to dynamically show correlations between progressed synastry aspects and events unfolding in the lives of real people.

For example, Westran says Prince Charles and Diana had a "hugely illustrative" set of progressed synastry aspects working during their time together, including the example above which shows Charles' progressing Venus forming a trine to Diana's progressing sun. The aspect helped define the early years of the relationship, but the storybook romance started to unravel after the progressed aspect became exact and started to wane. The marriage was officially over by the time it was no longer operative (in orb).

The newest Royal couple, William and Kate, caught a celestial break with a rare, long-lived progressed synastry trine aspect involving Kate's progressed Venus and William's natal Venus. The aspect is long-lived because Kate's progressed Venus was retrograde (traveling backwards in the heavens from our earth-bound point of view) when the couple met in 2000, and only began moving slowly forward in 2004. At its current pace, the progressed synastry aspect will not separate until 2030, at which time the couple will be able to rely upon other helpful aspects in both their natal and progressed synastry charts.

Westran believes progressed aspects provide a fertile field for future research efforts. For example, a promising new study looks at dynamic connections between the sun and Mars in the progressed charts of world leaders. Historically, the years 1922 and 1949 were significant for Stalin and Mao because they came to power in the USSR and China as progressed Mars advanced to form a conjunction with their natal sun. But a Mars/sun connection also was in play when Churchill, Truman, both Castro brothers, Mussolini and others came to power in their respective countries.

New Study Confirms Gauquelin Plus Zones

By Edward Snow

When in the last century French statistician Michael Gauquelin published the results of his ground-breaking statistical studies examining some basic tenets of astrology response from the academic community was anything but kind.

Gauquelin's work extended over a period of 23 years between 1949 and 1973. In a series of studies he statistically tested how the planets influenced everything from character traits to heredity, athletic prowess and the career paths taken by professionals who are eminent in their fields. Mostly, it was the studies dealing with eminent professionals and elite athletes that created such a ruckus in the scientific community.

Initially, in a study involving 508 births, Gauquelin impressively demonstrated a correlation of Mars and Saturn with physicians at a chance level in the millions to one range. Simply, in the birth charts of prominent physicians, Saturn or Mars were either rising or culminating in so-called Gauquelin "plus zones" with a significantly greater frequency than expected by chance.

One of the Gauquelin plus zones straddles what astrologers call the ascendant or rising sign on the birth chart's eastern horizon. Another hugs what astronomers call the meridian plane and astrologers refer to as the midheaven. Traditionally, planets posited near these "angles" in a birth chart are believed to express their influence more powerfully in the individual's life. Gauquelin had similar success correlating other professions with the planets traditionally identified with them. For example, Mars turned up in the plus zones for elite athletes, Saturn was there for scientists, the Moon for writers and Jupiter for actors and politicians. The significance level for some of these correlations was also in the millions to one chance level. However, this result applied only to eminent professionals and elite athletes and was not present in the birth charts of ordinary athletes or professionals who were not eminent in their fields, which gave critics some contentious talking points.

Canines to the Rescue

Michael Gauquelin is not the only researcher to demonstrate that planets rising on the Eastern horizon or culminating near the midheaven are more influential. A novel study by another French scientist, the late Prof. Suzel Fuzeau-Braesch of Paris University, sought to determine whether the behavior of 500 pedigreed puppies from 100 different litters would measurably correlate to rising or culminating planets in their birth charts. She was advised in this unique project by Michael's wife, Francoise Gauquelin, a statistician who also was closely involved with her husband in his work.

The whelping of a litter of puppies can extend over a period of several hours with as little as 15 minutes—or as much as two hours—between births. So birth charts lay out differently for every pup in a litter. The pups were closely monitored through the first eight weeks of life, but the hypothesized results were apparent almost immediately. Prof. Fuzeau-Braesch discovered that the dominant pups—the more aggressive, assertive, tail-wagging leaders of every group—had either the Sun or Jupiter rising or culminating in their birth charts with a frequency that far exceeded the threshold of significance established for the test.

Depending upon whatever else is going on in the heavens at the time, astrologers might describe humans with these same prominent planetary placements as charismatic, dominant, strong, sociable or influential. And psychologists might use the term extrovert when labeling these same essentially positive, outgoing personality traits. At Johnson State College in

Vermont, Psychology and Counseling Professor David Fink studied the Gauquelin results and came up with an ingenious way to test whether planets in the plus zones could predict introversion-extraversion behavioral traits as measured by the Eysenck Personality Inventory (EPI) questionnaire.

Prof. Fink directs Johnson State College's master's program in counseling. He first encountered Gauquelin's research in the 1980s and describes his interest in the statistician's work in this way:

"My field is the training of counselors and psychotherapists. We are vitally interested in any tool that helps us understand people and the challenging issues that bring them to seek help in therapy. The Gauquelin research stimulated my interest in examining whether the astrological birth chart might prove useful as an empirically defensible tool for assessing personality dimensions."

A More Promising Approach

Rather than testing the birth data of eminent professionals, Prof. Fink found a more promising—and less controversial—way to test the Gauquelin plus zones. Over a period of 15 years he administered EPI tests to 932 college students at three universities: Johnson State, the University of Vermont and the University of Maine. He was especially interested in the EPI test's "E" scale, which is a measure of introversion-extraversion. A high score on the "E" scale equates to extraversion and a low score to introversion.

Astrologers associate the planet Jupiter with expansive, outgoing personality traits and Saturn with caution and reserve. Prof. Fink hypothesized that individuals with Jupiter in one of the plus zones identified by Gauquelin should test higher on the "E" scale while those with Saturn in these locations should test lower.

To analyze the collected data he reached out to astrological researcher David Cochrane, who at the time was enrolled in graduate classes in research methodology and statistics at the University of Florida. Cochrane is a past president of the International Society for Astrological Research (ISAR) and is chairman and founder of the Cosmic Patterns astrological software company. At Florida University he got approval from the head of the Research and Evaluation Methodology Department to do the analysis as partial fulfillment for a three-credit independent study course. A professor in the sociology department, Monika Ardelt, mentored the project, providing "important suggestions that improved analysis of the results," he said.

A Statistically Significant Result

"Statistical significance is the gold standard for an experimental design that evaluates whether a hypothesis is true or not. A result is generally regarded as being statistically significant if the probability of obtaining it is less than 5 percent, or what researchers call a p value of .05. Researchers should collect enough data to potentially obtain this level of significance," Cochrane explained.

He points out that the placement of Jupiter or Saturn in one of the plus zones is only one variable among a great many possible astrological variables that might affect the "E" score. Also, non-astrological factors like genetics and the environment may factor into the outcome as well. With 982 cases, the researchers wanted to determine whether the effect of a single variable could be detected. It was.

"The result for this data analysis, which is known in statistics as a 2-tailed t-test, was significant at the .05 p value level. In a more sophisticated test that included age as a predictor of the E score the result was even better with a 2 percent probability. Effectively, the hypothesis was clearly stated and was confirmed by the result. Because the students did not know how Prof. Fink would analyze the data at the time they were tested there was no way for their test scores to have been influenced by the hypothesis tested," he added.

According to Prof. Fink, if results of the research eventually are replicated in future studies with a similar design the significance will be twofold. For one thing, it will present to scientists in other fields suggestive evidence of the birth chart's validity that will be difficult to dismiss out of hand without further serious investigation. Also, it will provide practicing astrologers with more precise guidelines for interpreting the strength of angular planets located in the Gauquelin plus zones.

Prof. Fink says his primary interest in the subject revolves around approaching astrology "as an alternative language system that can help clinicians assess and conceptualize their clients with different terminology, and also communicate with clients in vocabulary that is less stigmatizing to them than the psychopathologizing categories we traditionally employ in the mental health field.

"I speak to my students about the study after first describing to them the ground breaking work of the Gauquelins, and the reluctance of most empirical scientists to engage with the Gauquelin results. Students are generally fascinated with the work, but at the same time are somewhat daunted by the statistical and methodological issues that inevitably must be addressed," he noted.

Gardening by the Moon: Tradition vs. Science

By Nick Kollerstrom, PhD

In recent decades experiments have shown that the metabolism of plants, indicated by such things as their water absorption or oxygen metabolism, responds considerably to the monthly lunar cycle. Two researchers at the University of Paris have shown that plant DNA changes in tune to this cycle. Trees have electric fields around them, measurable by the potential gradient up the trunk. Ralph Markson in the United States monitored this for years and showed how fortnightly and monthly lunar rhythms were present.

Animal oestrus (coming-on-heat) is cyclic, and yet traditions link animal fertility to the lunar cycle. In the 2nd century AD, the astronomer Claudius Ptolemy reported of the practical, hard-headed farmers of the Roman Empire that they notice the aspects of the Moon, when at full, in order to direct the copulation of their herds and flocks, and the setting of plants or sowing of seeds. There is not an individual who considers these general precautions as impossible or unprofitable.

I have collected some years of data from a Thoroughbred stud farm, with dates of covering (bringing the stallion to the mare) plus recorded conceptions. Mating takes place within just a few months in the spring of each year, which makes investigating the lunar cycle influence tricky. Yet this data does clearly seem to show both increased fertility and increased coming-on-heat on the days around and just after the Full Moon. If correct, this could have practical implications for horse breeding.

These investigations don't always support traditional folklore in this area, but they tend to suggest that there is something in it. They are relevant to beliefs such as that some part of the lunar month is best for pruning trees, i.e., the waning half, while the waxing half if better for grafting; or that calves should not be gelded around the Full Moon.

Applying the Theories

Do seeds germinate better at some point of the lunar cycle? My experiments with seeds grown at constant temperature tended to confirm the results published by Lilly Kolisko in the late 1930s, namely that seeds would usually germinate better if sown around the full Moon, and especially on the day or two prior to it.

There were some experiments conducted around 1940 by the John Innes Foundation, reported in what was then the Journal of the Royal Horticultural Society (RHS), to test Kolisko's claims. My view is that their results did in fact support Kolisko's findings, but the report averred the contrary, prejudice against such notions being rather strong at that time. Kolisko, who had emigrated from Germany in the 1930s, became disillusioned with the negative response to her research.

The vital question of how final crop yield is affected by sowing date has been thoroughly investigated within the bio-dynamic movement. However, deep disagreement exists amongst experts in this area. For some decades now, Maria Thun has been reporting her results in her yearly Moon calendar, which apparently show weight-yields in accord with the elements of the sidereal or star-zodiac.

We are here asked to envisage four steps of crop growth: first the root (Earth), then the leafy shoots (Water) then the flowers with their airy fragrance (Air) and lastly the summer's heat dries up the crop, maturing the seed (Fire). Crops can be viewed as belonging to one of these elements, depending on whether they are a root, leaf, flower, or fruit/seed crop. From this it follows that there is a proper lunar timetable appropriate for each crop. For instance, potatoes, as a root-crop, grow best when they are sown as the Moon is passing in front of earth-element constellations (in the astrological zodiac).

This is, the pragmatic may object, more like some alchemical mandala than a scientific theory. It is indeed simple, but does it work? Is it really worthwhile—or indeed practical—for farmers to organize their work schedule around it?

In 1975, together with a market gardener, I started to test the theory, by successive crop rows sown over a lunar month. Since then, British experiments on the topic have involved about five hundred rows sown of diverse vegetables. I have published many of these results, and have reviewed the researches of others. My view is that the theory stands up, and that Empedocles could not improve on it.

Not Everyone Agrees

A weighty German bio-dynamic textbook makes skeptical references to the Thun-model: the stars do not affect crop yields they say. In view of the diversity of opinion on this matter, and the diverging instructions given in the lunar-gardening guides now on sale, we should perhaps consider more how plant growth varies in accord with the green fingers and even the expectations of the sower.

The Secret Life of Plants by Tompkins and Bird wasn't just a hippy pipe-dream of the sixties, and plants are sensitive in ways we tend not to give them credit for. But folklore ends and science begins when results are obtained that are repeatable. Replications of the Thun effect—the classic Thun and Heinze results published in the early seventies describing eight years of potato-yields (1964-71) are in my view sufficiently substantial for some such claim to be made.

Each year about one hundred thousand copies of the Thun calendar are sold world-wide, in 21 different languages. The aim here has been to introduce the notion that all living things, including us, respond to the motions of the moon. For growers to use a calendar based upon the moon may be a sensible idea.

Long ago, at the very dawn of British culture, before even Stonehenge, there were two stone circles at the heart of Avebury. Both a hundred meters across, one was comprised of 29 huge stones and the other of

27. These signified the two fundamental lunar cycles, as used today in a lunar gardening calendar. They turn against each other: the 27-day orbit period, and its 29-day waxing and waning cycle. Did Britons learn to count from these cycles? Other cycles too are woven into a Moon calendar, and we can feel the turning of the wheel of life by using it through the seasons.

How Astrologers Measure the Night Sky

By Robert Currey

When we look up at a clear starlit night sky we are gazing at a magnificent four-dimensional panorama. The crescent moon and the planets are set against the backdrop of a multitude of illuminated specks. Each wandering star (as planets were termed by the ancient Greeks) can be tracked in two dimensions above and below the projected path of the Sun, which is known as the ecliptic.

To a limited extent, through a process known as stellar parallax, it is possible to gauge a third dimension—the distance visually from the earth. And we also view the starry spectacle in the fourth dimension of time. This is because, from our vantage point on earth, the more distant planets are within *light-hours* while visible stars can be more than a thousand *light-years* away. In one sense, some stellar patterns may no longer exist in the form we see them on Earth today.

While astronomers can pinpoint the orbital elements of these celestial objects with great precision, most astrologers work in only two dimensions. Astrologers locate the planets by their position along the path of the Sun or the ecliptic and most ignore height above or below the ecliptic since most planets are within 3.5 degrees. This one spatial dimension is complemented by the dimension of time, which is measured by the orbital period of the Sun relative to the Earth.

Do Astrologers Ignore Distance?

Critics point out that astrologers fail to take account of planetary distance. They argue that no adjustment is made for the great variation in the distances between, say, Mars and the Earth. Or they argue Pluto is so distant that it should have no more than a negligible effect.

This flaw so irked Paul Kurtz, a philosophy professor from Buffalo, New York, that he and his colleagues persuaded 186 leading astronomers and other scientists to sign a highly critical statement about astrology. The letter published in the *Humanist* in 1975 and included this comment:

"In ancient times people...had no concept of the vast distances from the earth to the planets and stars. Now that these distances can and have been calculated, we can see how infinitesimally small are the gravitational and other effects produced by the distant planets and the far more distant stars."

Astronomer Carl Sagan, host of the award-winning TV series *Cosmos*, refused to sign the statement because he found the tone authoritarian, and the grounds insufficient. He wrote "*No mechanism was known for continental drift when it was proposed.*" All the great geophysicists at the time who were certain that continents were fixed were later proved wrong by the theory of plate tectonics.

At the time, astrologer Al Morrison wrote to all the signatories on behalf of the Congress of Astrological Organizations, publisher of the CAO Times, asking each of the 181 male and five female scientists: "A*s an authority in both science and astrology,* where were their experiments and evaluations that led them to this conclusion were published. Not one scientist was prepared to justify their statement. Kurtz, however went on to found the sceptical organization CSICOP (now known as CSI) and unwittingly provided some of the best evidence to support astrology, but that's another story.

Distances Not a Problem

There are four reasons why planetary distances are not a problem for astrology:

1. Cycles and Transits. The speed of a planet orbiting the Sun is determined by its distance from the Sun. So a distant planet like Nep-

tune travels both slower and over a longer orbit than Mercury, which zooms closely around the Sun by comparison. In 2012, Correlation journal published a simple formula in which this author combined Kepler's Third Law with Euclidean geometry. It sets out how the distance from the Sun, the orbital period and the speed of each planet are all in the same proportion.

Consequently, the most distant outer planets have long ranging slow cycles. Astrologers interpret their movements in a natal chart on a generational and collective level. For example Neptune may reveal how an individual fits in with the ideals of their generation. In addition, the length of a transit varies according to the speed of a planet. A transit of the Moon lasts around four hours and a Neptune transit lasts around two and a half years.

2. Retrograde Planets. Besides tracking planetary cycles and transits, astrologers take account of distance in yet another way. An Ephemeris (planetary tables) log the periods when each planet travels retrograde. Retrograde motion is when a planet temporarily appears from Earth to be travelling backwards. Venus and Mercury only travel retrograde when closest to the Earth. When Mercury is retrograde, astrologers consider it as a time to rethink, review, rewrite and even reroute journeys.

When any of the planets beyond the Earth's orbit (such as Mars or Pluto) travel retrograde they are on the near side of the Sun and therefore closer to the Earth than when their motion is direct. Some astrologers adapt their interpretation specifically for a retrograde planet. But all will notice on the birth chart that the planet is in the opposite hemisphere to the Sun, Mercury, Venus and often Mars in the birth chart. This alignment tends to result in planetary oppositions, which require a particular interpretation.

3. Relevant Distance. Is a quantity such as distance relevant to astrology at all? Even though astrologers take distance into account in so many techniques, is distance so critical in astrological practice? Scientists work with quantitative data, so distances for them are a vital statistic. Astrologers place emphasis on qualitative planetary properties such as archetypes, which do not vary according to distance.

4. The Scientific Objection. Of course, the first three reasons still leave

the scientific objection—how can astrology work over such distances? When critics claim that distant planets are too weak to have any influence, they assume astrology can only work by a force that is governed by the Inverse Square Law.

Newton's Law states that the strength of a radiating force or energy such as gravity, electromagnetism or sound is inversely proportional to the distance from the source. Yet our understanding of these forces is far from complete. In particular, gravity appears to have a number of unexplained anomalies. Within our solar system resonance has the effect of enhancing forces such as gravity even over considerable distances. In a paper published in *Correlation* in 2013 entitled "Our Solar Matrix," this author detailed how gravitational resonance has led to a pattern of significant ratios and geometrical relationships between planetary orbits. A possible mechanism for this high level of interconnectivity within the solar system, termed astrotaxis, was proposed.

The wide-ranging application of astrology suggests that, like weather patterns, it may be subject to the mix of several complex mechanisms.

One possibility comes from the field of quantum physics. Experiments in China in 2012 have shown how two separated atoms can be entangled in such a way that a signal is generated over distances of up to 97 kilometres. Austrian quantum physicist Professor Aspelmeyer speculated that quantum entanglement could occur over much larger distances in space.

In 1958 Carl Jung, in collaboration with theoretical physicist Wolfgang Pauli, published his theory of synchronicity. This model based on the quality of time rather than the quantity of space has become popular among astrologers. With synchronicity, distance is irrelevant.

Even models based on conventional physics, such as those of astronomer Percy Seymour, involve all the planets in the solar system despite the huge distances. He writes that: "...the movement of the Sun about the common centre of mass of the Solar System is controlled by the orbiting of the outer planets: Jupiter, Saturn, Neptune and Uranus."

Dr Seymour continues: "All the planets at various stages of the solar cycle will through their tidal tug on the magnetic canals of the Sun, contribute to the triggering of sunspot activity. At the start of the cycle, the conjunction of Mercury and Venus will play a major role."

Fluctuations in the solar cycle lead to variations in the geomagnetic field via the solar wind, resulting in biological and other consequences on Earth.

It is understandable that critics are inclined to believe that a measuring system that was established some two thousand years ago should be inappropriate given today's superior technology. Remarkably, it turns out that the two dimensional geocentric model of the solar system is sufficiently comprehensive for most astrological applications. What is less understandable are those who obstruct scientific research by ignoring the lessons of history.

So many discoveries, such as the compass, gravity, the battery and aspirin, have all been of value without knowing how they work. In some cases the evidence is hard to demonstrate. Researchers who discovered the transmission of germs, plate tectonics or the link between smoking and cancer were dismissed and ridiculed for years by so-called experts. So it is unwise and not good scientific practice to dismiss astrology on the basis that the mechanism is not yet known.

References

Aspelmeyer, et al. "Long-Distance Free-Space Distribution of Quantum Entanglement," *Science*, 2003, pp. 301, 621-623.

Currey, Robert. "Our Solar Matrix," *Correlation*, Vol. 29, 2013, pp. 5-38.

Currey, Robert. "A Formula for Orbital Synthesis," *Correlation*, Vol. 28, 2013.

Ertel, Suitbert. "Appraisal of Shawn Carlson's Renowned Astrology Tests," *Journal of Scientific Exploration*, Vol. 23, 2009, pp. 125-137.

Euclid (ca. 300 BC). *Elements*, Proposition 2 of Book XII. "Circles are to one another as the squares on their diameters."

Fraknoi, Andrew. *The Universe At Your Fingertips Activity: Activities With Astrology*, Astronomical Society of the Pacific, 2012.

Jung, C.G. and W. Pauli, C.A. Meier, ed., David Roscoe, trans. *Atom and Archetype: The Pauli/Jung Letters. 1932-1958*, Princeton University Press, 2001.

Kepler, Johannes. *Harmonices Mundi* [Harmony of the World], 1619.

Kurtz, Paul, Bart Bok, Lawrence Jerome, et al. *Objections to Astrology*. Jointly published by the American Ethical Union and the American Humanist Association, 1975.

McRitchie, Ken. "Support for Astrology from the Carlson Double-blind Experiment." Astrology News Service, 2011.
Minkel, J.R. "Quantum Spookiness Spans the Canary Islands," Scientific American, July 6, 2012, Vol. 337, pp. 72-75. Researcher envisions beaming entangled photons into space. Physicist Anton Zeilinger of the University of Vienna says. "I am dreaming of an experiment where you do it [entanglement experiment] between Earth and [the] moon," March 9, 2007.
Rosenfeld, W., et al. "Heralded Entanglement Between Widely Separated Atoms," *Science* July 6, 2012, Vol. 337, pp. 72-75
Seymour, Percy. "The Scientific Proof of Astrology," *Quantum*, 1997, pp.176-177.
Yin, Juan, et al. "Teleporting Independent Qubits Through a 97 km Freespace Channel," *Nature* 388, 2012, pp.185-188.

The Lunar Cycle and the Economy

By Edward Snow

While the Great Depression of the 1930s dragged on, a business astrologer described a method for predicting long-term economic trends that continues to produce spot-on results in the current era.

In a book published almost 80 years ago, financial astrologer and author Louise McWhirter described her theory of business cycles and suggested the low point for the economy had already been reached in 1933—when the Great Depression was at its lowest ebb. She also predicted the next peak in economic activity was years away: November 1942.

McWhirter historically tracked cyclical ups and downs in the economy for 100 years, beginning in 1850. Given the times, her depression-era prediction that the economy would reach a new cyclical high point late in 1942 may not have seemed to promise much. However, the predicted cyclical turnaround turned out to be dynamic as it coincided with the massive economic stimulus spending set in motion by the build-up for World War II.

The Next Economic Peak?

In the current era, financial astrologer Grace K. Morris, MA, LPMAFA, used McWhirter's predictive methods to accurately determine the economy would hit bottom in 2008 and start a gradual climb back to normalcy

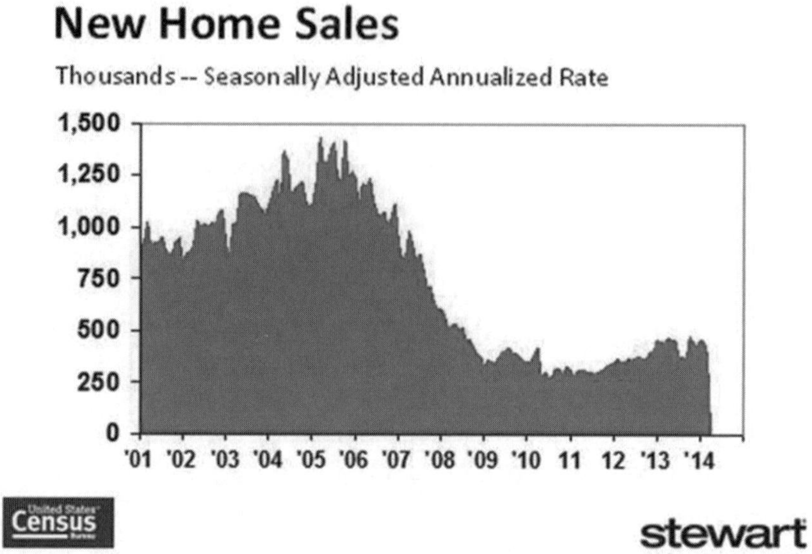

a year later. As Morris surmised, by 2012 economic performance was improving as part of an upward trend that is not expected to peak until 2017. So, at this point, we're still a few years away from the next significant economic downturn.

In her book, *Astrology and Stock Market Forecasting,* McWhirter describes the correlation she discovered between economic activity and the 18.6-year lunar cycle defined by the Moon's transiting nodes. The nodes are sensitive points in space that are astronomically determined by the moon's orbit around the earth and the earth's apparent path around the sun—the ecliptic.

The north and south nodes are always 180 degrees apart in opposing astrological signs. In tandem, they travel backwards through the zodiac in counter-clockwise fashion. The ascending north node is always rising above the ecliptic and the south node descending below it.

In studying the connection between the Moon's nodes and economic activity, McWhirter consistently found the north node in the sign of Aquarius during periods of low economic activity. At the halfway point in the 18.6-year cycle, the north node is moving into the sign of Leo, where economic high points have historically been recorded. After this, the long-term trend ratchets lower as the north node slowly and deliberately makes its way back to the sign of Aquarius, where the cycle begins anew.

What About Housing?

Astrologer Alice Reichard describes a similar study that looked at highs and lows for the housing market. Her study tracked data dating to the Civil War and also found a correlation between the transiting lunar nodes and cyclical highs and lows in the housing market. The housing cycle begins from a different starting point and typically leads the economic cycle into the next recovery period.

In August 2009, Morris said the north node moved into the sign of Capricorn, which is where Reichard predicted the low point for housing would be. Only this time around the market was severely overheated and the downside was particularly turbulent with falling home prices and foreclosures at levels not seen since the Great Depression.

Today the housing market in the U.S. is in recovery mode but is not expected to peak until 2020. That's when the north node will be arriving in Cancer, the astrological sign identified with domesticity and matters related to hearth and home.

Both the financial and housing markets are influenced by cycles within cycles. And long-term progress invariably is made in fits and starts. Obviously, the fiscal policies of governments can also help or hinder the way each cycle unwinds.

For example, in 2007, the housing market was supposed to be winding down as it approached a cyclical low. Instead, in the U.S., it was racing along at high speed with an under-regulated financial industry awash in capital it couldn't wait to lend to unqualified borrowers. When it came the adjustment was abrupt and pernicious—and right on schedule, Morris said.

The economic bubble that developed in the housing industry in 2007 precipitated the economic collapse that followed in 2008. With the Moon's north node poised to roll into the no-nonsense sign of Capricorn it would have been far better had bankers honored this development by exercising more caution and fiscal restraint, she added.

Another example of policies interfering with cycles can be observed by contrasting economic developments in Europe and the U.S. following the Great Recession that began in 2008. The Moon's nodal influence is the same everywhere but policymakers in Europe chose a different way to deal with economic contraction.

The Europeans opted for the kind of austerity program that may have been a better option earlier in the cycle. The U.S. chose to stimulate the economy with apparently better results. However, if history repeats in the broadly general way it usually does there's a very good chance that global economies will all be expanding when the north node returns once again to the generous sign of Leo.

Study Connects Divorce Rates with Planetary Patterns

By Edward Snow

As star-crossed lovers go, Romeo and Juliet had nothing on Burton and Taylor, the charismatic motion picture stars who sizzled on the silver screen in Joseph Mankiewicz's Cleopatra, Shakespeare's Taming of the Shrew and Albee's *Who's Afraid of Virginia Wolf?* before flaming out in a real-life romance as spectacularly incendiary as any Tinseltown has seen.

The attraction between them was so strong that two of Elizabeth Taylor's eight marriages were to Richard Burton. And the actors each believed the other to be the love of their lives.

Research astrologer and couples expert Alexandra Mark says a study she conducted years ago with the late Harvard University statistician John P. Gilbert, PhD, linked Burton and Taylor to a celestial pattern that turns up more frequently than expected by chance in married couples with staying power. Couples with this particular planetary combination are in marriages that end in divorce less frequently than couples that don't have it in their compared birth charts (horoscopes).

"Professor Gilbert was more than skeptical of astrology; he was downright hostile. But he agreed to design the test and handle the statistical analysis because he apparently believed that astrology would fail and be discredited."

"It was difficult for him to hide his disappointment when the testing twice produced statistically significant positive results for astrology. Replicating the original finding in a more tightly controlled "double-blind" follow-up test was important because it added strength to the argument that the result is not an aberration," she noted.

Mark is a graduate of Boston University and has a PhD in comparative literature from Boston College. She has been a consulting astrologer since the 1970s and is the author of two books on the subject, *Astrology for the Aquarian Age* and *Marriage: Made in Heaven.*

Her article, "Sun-Moon and Venus-Mars Ties as a Prognosticator in Divorce: A Statistical Study," published in *The Mountain Astrologer* magazine. Mark says the study of what brings couples together or causes them to fly or drift apart has been the major focus of her astrological practice. Modern statistical techniques make it possible to test some vary old theories, she suggests.

To predict compatibility and attraction, astrologers compare the natal birth charts of couples using a technique known as synastry, which establishes and evaluates the way the Sun, Moon and planets in the respective birth charts align with each other. Although a plausible physical explanation for why the technique works has yet to surface, rigorously analyzed statistical data supports its viability, she maintains.

Evaluating the Aspects

Traditionally, in synastry comparisons, some angular relationships or "aspects" are presumed to be more powerful than others. This especially applies to the conjunction, which in a synastry comparison occurs when the Sun, Moon or a planet from one chart is in roughly the same degree of a zodiacal sign as the Sun, Moon or a planet in the chart with which it is being compared. The opposition aspect, which spaces the compared planets roughly 180 celestial degrees apart in opposite zodiacal signs, is considered to be a powerful aspect as well.

When describing synastry, most astrological textbooks stress the importance of strong Sun-Moon ties between couples. In her practice, Mark says she has found that strong Sun-Moon aspects correlate with friendship on a deeply emotional level—the couples who think of themselves as being "best friends." It doesn't matter if it is his Sun and her Moon or the other way around. It works either way.

The other part of the marriage equation is the physical attraction or sexual "chemistry" everyone hopes to find. The possibility for personal "fireworks" of this sort is indicated by the way Mars and Venus are aligned in the synastry chart, she explained.

Mark points out that Taylor and Burton can be counted among a relatively small group of couples who not only have a strong Sun-Moon connection in their synastry charts but a dynamic Mars -Venus alignment as well. In the couples population, this double whammy occurs randomly about 10 percent of the time, or roughly once in every 10 marriages.

For Burton and Liz, the combination was more powerful than for most because both his and her Sun and Moon were involved in close aspects with each other, and his Mars and her Venus were aligned by opposition. They were friends on a deeply emotional level but there also was a strong physical attraction that kept things stirred up.

Although the famous couple was twice married and divorced, their will to be together was exceptional. And they defied every convention to follow their hearts, she observes.

A Testable Hypothesis

In the modern era, marriages don't last as long as they once did. However, Mark theorized that couples with both Sun-Moon and Mars-Venus ties in their synastry charts would spend less time in divorce court than couples whose synastry charts weren't aligned in this way.

Gilbert agreed that this was a testable hypothesis. Over a period three years, two tests involving hundreds of couples were completed.

For the "double-blind" second test, Gilbert obtained birth data for 446 divorced couples from public records and had this information shipped directly to him at Harvard, where it was organized by assistants. For comparison purposes, the statistician created an equal number of computer-generated imaginary couples, who were electronically "born" in the same years as the real divorced couples.

Mark prepared synastry charts for both the real and imaginary couples without knowing which was which. When the comparison charts were completed, the information was sent to Gilbert for analysis.

Simply, if her theory about Sun-Moon and Mars-Venus ties was wrong, the number of real divorced couples with this combination would be statistically indistinguishable from the random, computer-generated imaginary pairs. But that's not what the statistician found when analyzing the data.

Although relatively small for both groups, the combination turned up less frequently among couples whose marriages ended in divorce. The percentage of couples with the Sun-Moon and Mars-Venus ties was almost twice as high as the control group, which represented the population as a whole.

"The odds were two in 100 that this outcome occurred by chance, which placed the result well within parameters defined by statisticians as being statistically significance," Mark said.

Astrology Researcher Accurately Predicts U.S. Elections

By Edward Snow

An astrological study has gone back in time to predict winners in the last 33 U.S. presidential elections with uncanny accuracy, including President Obama's victories in the 2008 and 2012 campaigns.

Nina Gryphon, an astrologer, investor and corporate attorney who works with high tech industry clients, says her research looked at U.S. elections dating back to 1880.

"But the traditional mundane predictive methods used in the research date to antiquity," she explained.

Gryphon has BA, MA and JD degrees from Stanford University and uses astrology to help clients find favorable times for business and investing.

"At its core, the technique and rules were first set down in writing by ancient Sumerians four millennia ago and probably date back much farther than that," she said.

In the current era, the researcher interpreted horoscopes created for the exact moment the sun entered the astrological sign of Aries in the nation's capital during election years. In the ancient world, similar charts were used to predict the fortunes of kings in power and those who might challenge or threaten the throne.

"The ancients thought of the Spring Equinox (when the sun arrives at zero Aries) as the yearly anniversary of the creation of the universe. It was viewed as the first moment of existence containing the seeds of the future unfolding through time.

"Persians today still celebrate this day as Nowruz, the New Year," she explained.

"So the theory has a respectable pedigree and seemed worthy of examination," she said.

In her study of U.S. elections Gryphon applied specific traditional rules regarding the placement and alignment of planets within the zero Aries horoscope wheel. Some planetary influences were identified with the incumbent or the incumbent's political party and others with the challenger.

"The planets of the winning party were found to have a connection with other strongly placed planets whereas the losing party's planets were either not doing anything or were being actively harmed by other planets. This is extremely basic astrology," she said.

Still, initially, the researcher was only able to successfully predict the outcome about 80 percent of the time.

"It was clear I wasn't seeing the whole picture but over time the rules pertaining to the remaining 20 percent of the horoscopes gradually began to reveal themselves.

"Given a random horoscope from my sample I'm now able to correctly predict the outcome 90 to 95 percent of the time. Any lack of accuracy I attribute to operator error," she said,

More to Astrology

But there's more to astrology than calling elections, Gryphon believes.

"In my experience there's a great demand for astrological advice in the financial and corporate worlds; one simply has to speak the right language. In any highly competitive sphere, people want to gain an advantage age over the competition.

"Our earliest texts indicate that astrology was developed to advise the rich and powerful. The early Babylonians spent considerable time watching the Sun and Venus specifically for information about the political and economic situation in the land," she points out.

Gryphon says financial astrology is one application for astrology that does not get much play in the public eye, yet it is extremely useful and frequently used. Many use astrology yet few will admit it publicly, partly because it is socially unacceptable to speak against the prevailing scientism but also because no one wants to give away their advantage.

"I've come to realize we live in two overlapping worlds. There's the world described in our public discourse, such as the news media, where things are portrayed as rational, scientific and measurable. And there's the world we actually live in, which motivates our decisions and which is far richer, more complicated and filled with things reason cannot explain," she said.

Pups in Paris Influenced by Planetary Alignments

By Edward Snow

No one who owns one doubts the family pooch exhibits personality traits that seem remarkably human at times. Is there a way to rationally explain this?

Award-winning French scientists Suzel Fuzeau-Braesch believes there is. In a series of research studies described in her book, *Astrology off the Beaten Path*, she provides convincing evidence that humans aren't the only species on the planet that are behaviorally impacted by where solar system planets turn up in their astrological birth charts.

Fuzeau-Braesch is an influential member of the prestigious Centre National de Recherche Scientifique in Paris and an honorary director of research for the National Center for Scientific Research (CERN) in France. She earned a Docteur d'Etates Sciences (D.Sc) from the University of Paris and, over a long and distinguished career, published best-selling books in France, authored 150 academic publications and earned various academic honors, including the prize known as the Gaveau de Kerville.

For 25 years she headed a research laboratory at University Paris XI-Orsay, where she researched animals' lifestyles, pigmentations and brain behavior biochemistry. And, to the chagrin of various skeptic groups, their susceptibility to astrological influences as well.

Initially a skeptic herself, Fuzeau-Braesch decided to test the accuracy and reliability of an astrological report writing system she chanced upon in an Oxford Street shop in London in 1970. Computerized report-writing systems produce detailed personality profiles based on birth data alone.

The scientist recalls being surprised by how "accurately and uncannily" the astrological profiles described some close family members. The experience triggered a decades-long effort to determine "if astrological tools and concepts could be confirmed by hard science."

After years of independent inquiry sandwiched between her regular teaching and research responsibilities, Fuzeau-Braesch founded Researches Astrologiques Methodes Scientifiques (RAMS) with colleagues in 1992 to collaborate on findings and publish an astrological research journal. She makes the point that astrology was "constructed" over the course of more than two millennia with the imprint of a variety of cultures and mythological beliefs. So an objective, open-minded approach is essential when applying scientific methods to the ancient craft.

Checking out how the discipline might apply to the behavior of animals is scientifically valid "because animals will act naturally and not be influenced by culture or preconceived ideas," she wrote.

Dog Breeders Lend a Hand

In her book Fuzeau-Braesch describes a five-year study that sought to determine whether the behavior of 500 purebred puppies closely observed through their first eight weeks of life was astrologically indicated by the way planets were aligned in the sky at the exact moment of birth. The study, which was published in the *Journal for Scientific Exploration*, involved 12 Paris area dog breeders and 15 different breeds—everything from tiny Chihuahuas to much larger Labs and German Shepherds.

Over the course of the study, 100 litters with between two and eight pups each were investigated. For economic reasons (customers typically want as much information as they can get) breeders routinely keep more detailed records for puppies than are kept for most children, including exact birth times for each pup, detailed physical descriptions and anecdotal stories describing the way each pup behaves and interacts with litter mates.

Breeders generally agree that behavioral traits are well established by the time the puppies can legally be sold after eight weeks. For the Paris study, breeders provided information in ordinary, non-technical language and the researchers organized it using the Eysenck method of expressing behavior as either extroversion or neuroticism.

Personality types were categorized as Active, Dominant, Reserved, Affectionate, Nervous, and Staid (stable) with numerous descriptive subtraits listed for each category. For example, under the Active category, the researchers included such traits as bold, rascally, daring, curious, and impudent. Dominant pups were aggressive, belligerent, strong willed, determined and boss of the litter, while pups in the reserved category were timorous, discrete, distant, solitary, shy and so on.

Because litter mates are usually born with the same Sun sign, projecting behavioral patterns based on simple Sun sign astrology wasn't an option. Instead, Fuzeau-Braesch designed the study to test the traditional astrological notion that planets found near the "angles" of the birth chart (within 10 degrees) more powerfully influence character and personality.

In astrology, the "angles" of a birth chart are on the eastern horizon where the Sun rises and on the western horizon where it sets. The other major angles are formed overhead at the highest point in the sky map (the Midheaven) and at the lowest (the Nadir).

From any vantage point on Earth the sky map is continually changing due to the earth's daily rotation on its axis. The Sun, Moon and planets independently arrive at each of the sensitive angles at some point during the day or night within a 24-hour period.

Fuzeau-Braesch thought testing the strength of planets at the angles using pedigreed pups was a credible approach because the staggered whelping of a puppy litter can extend over a period of several hours with as little as 15 minutes—and as much as two hours—between individual births. The sky map above and below the horizon is continually changing as the birthing process unfolds, setting up a different astrological dynamic for each individual pup.

An Amazing Finding

In what she described as an "amazing finding," the researcher discovered that dominant dogs—the leaders of every group—had the Sun and Jupiter in angular positions with a frequency that far exceeded the threshold of significance established for the test.

In human astrology, people born with these placements are generally described as charismatic, dominant, strong, sociable and influential. In the canine world, the pups with these placements were often first to eat and the entire group accepted this. Also, they would push the others away to get the attention of humans or just to move around. "This parallel is remarkable and cannot be due to chance," she suggested.

Fuzeau-Braesch said the study also produced other positive though less impressive statistically significant results; for example, a reserved character with Saturn prominently positioned at one of the angles. But a larger sample would be needed to confirm these results statistically with greater confidence, she admitted.

The scientist also described a much smaller study involving 30 cloned cows that produced similar results. Despite having identical heredity, the cloned cows were born at different times and developed individual patterns of behavior that "correspond perfectly with classical astrological laws."

So far, no other scientific explanation (other than astrology) has been proposed to explain this observed difference in behavior, she noted.

Astronomers Finding Evidence for Astrological Claims

By Edward Snow

Skeptics may find this a hard pill to swallow, but astronomers have done more than anyone to demonstrate the validity of the ancient belief system underpinning astrology.

In an article for *The National*, the leading English-language newspaper in the Middle East, author Robert Matthews says there no longer is any doubt that celestial bodies affect our planet as a whole.

Matthews is a visiting reader in science at Aston University in Birmingham, England. He says these links go beyond the obvious, such as the role of the sun and moon in the tides.

"The biggest climatic upheavals experienced by our planet are now known to be under the influence of the other planets in our solar system," he says.

Through their gravitational tugging, the moon and planets distort the shape of the Earth's orbit and the tilt of its axis to its orbit, causing subtle changes in the intensity of sunlight reaching us.

"By altering the level of heating reaching different latitudes, these changes are now thought to play a key role in triggering the huge expansion in polar ice characteristic of an Ice Age," he explains.

"Now astronomers think they may have uncovered another astrological connection between the Earth and its fellow planets—one that beggars the trivia of astrology.."

More than 150 years ago astronomers noticed that the number of sunspots appearing on the solar disk followed a distinct pattern, rising and falling over a period of about 11 years. This is curiously close to the 11.9 years that it takes Jupiter, the biggest planet in the solar system, to complete one orbit of the sun.

"It's hard to know what to make of such coincidences. But in 1852 the Swiss astronomer Johann Wolf showed that despite its great distance Jupiter had more gravitational effect on the sun than any other planet," Mathews said.

Theory Postulated

Wolf went on to develop a theory that seemed to account for sunspot numbers via the influence of Jupiter and other planets. However, because sunspots are a symptom of solar activity, and this in turn directly affects the earth, Wolf's ideas "sounded uncomfortably close to astrology," Mathews said.

He speculates that this is probably the reason why Wolf's ideas were hastily dumped at the start of the 20th century following the discovery of a link between sunspots and the magnetic field of the sun.

For whatever reason, Wolf's evidence linking the gravity of planets with the magnetic field of the sun wasn't believed to be compelling. But a team led by Dr. Jose Abreu of the ETH Zurich Institute for Geophysics in Switzerland has rekindled the controversy with impressive new evidence for precisely such a link.

To make its case, the team examined records of solar activity far more extensive than those used by Wolf, who could only go back as far as the mid-17th century and the first telescopic observations of sunspots by Galileo.

Dr. Abreu and his colleagues exploited the fact that changes in the sun's magnetic field affect the levels of cosmic rays smashing into the earth's atmosphere—which in turn creates isotopes that get trapped in polar ice and tree rings.

By analyzing the rise and fall in levels of these isotopes the team was able to reconstruct the peaks and troughs in solar activity covering more than 9,000 years,

"Armed with so much data the team has been able to look for patterns in the activity far more subtle than those found by Wolf. And what they have found broadly confirms his idea of a planetary influence on the sun," Mathews said.

Published in the current issue of *Astronomy & Astrophysics,* the team's findings stress that the planets cannot be the prime driver for the 11-year cycle of solar sunspot activity. If that were so, the orbits of the planets would change noticeably through the energy needed to drive the activity.

"But the planets can and do seem capable of affecting the processes that generate the sun's magnetic field," Mathews says.

Analysis of the isotope data has uncovered a set of cycles of solar activity ranging from about 85 to more than 500 years, each of which appears to be linked to planetary cycles.

Effect Is Dynamic

"This sounds pretty esoteric until one ponders the implications. Every so often, these cycles combine to produce periods of especially high or low activity. When this happens the effect on the earth can be dynamic," he noted.

Astronomers have identified several periods in recent history when unusually high or low solar activity coincided with anomalous conditions on earth. Among them is the Medieval Warm Period lasting from about 1000 to 1250. And the so-called Little Ice Age, which lasted, roughly, between 1350 to 1850.

Each coincides with peaks and troughs in solar activity triggered by the planets, and to events of major historical significance. For example, the bitter winters of the Little Ice Age caused mass starvation and social upheaval in Europe during the 16th and 17th centuries.

"The emerging evidence for planets influencing the sun and thereby global events suggests that the real problem with astrology is that its claims were simply too modest," Mathews concludes.

Can Astrology Bring You a Baby?

By Edward Snow

An online program designed to help medical professionals swiftly identify optimal dates for fertility treatments based on astrological indications may be coming soon to a clinic near you.

Astrologer Pat Harris, PhD, reports that a system based on ground-breaking research she completed for her doctorate thesis at the University of Southampton, UK, is in the early development stage. The research, titled *Applications of Astrology to Health Psychology: Astrological Factors and Fertility Treatment Outcomes*, successfully demonstrated that certain angular relationships of Venus and Jupiter to planets in a woman's natal birth chart can identify those years in a woman's life when she is more likely to bear children.

The research makes it easier for interested patients and clinicians to incorporate astrology into fertility treatment plans. Women can now find optimal dates for successful conception—with or without assisted reproductive technology (ART).

Dr. Harris is editor of *Correlations*, a journal published by the Astrological Association of Great Britain (AA). She also earned a masters degree in health psychology from the University of Southampton, and has been a consulting astrologer for more than 30 years.

"I have clients who have been with me for more than 20 years who keep returning for life management advice. Some would ask if they would marry and have children and when this would be. I used traditional astrology to locate the years when there was a strong likelihood of these events happening in their lives.

"Astrology didn't let me down as I had considerable success with these forecasts for natural conceptions," she said.

Dr. Harris says a decision to look at astrology and fertility treatment outcomes was made because the treatment process is stressful and invasive as well as being expensive. And because the rate of success is poor—only one in four in the UK.

"If a new method could be found to reduce the number of treatments needed to succeed this would be invaluable in every way to women who hope to have children through assisted reproductive technology," she added.

In an interview with the Astrology News Service (ANS) Dr. Harris provided the following insights:

ANS: Can astrology bring you a baby?

Dr. Harris: Based on my research I believe the answer to this question is a very clear yes. Clinicians may wish to consider use of astrology to select dates for embryo implantation because of its potential to increase the likelihood of a successful outcome. However, it is very important that the patient understands that astrological indicators do not guarantee success. My research shows only that attempts to conceive during optimal times have an increased likelihood of success (the birth of a live baby) compared with attempts made when the indicators are not present. It should also be made clear to patients that the absence of favorable astrological indicators means only that the chances of succeeding may be lower and does not portend a failed outcome.

ANS: When and how was your research carried out?

Dr. Harris: Between 2000 and 2002 I collected data from woman volunteers in the U.S., Australia and the UK who had undergone fertility treatment and were willing to let me explore their outcomes. I looked at the volunteers' birth charts and the dates at which they underwent embryo transfers, including IVF (in vitro fertilization); ICSI (intra-cytoplasm sperm injection); IUI (donor insemination); and other forms of treatment, such as GIFT (gamete intra-fallopian transfer) and ZIFT (zygote intra-fallopian transfer).

For the study I used a very sophisticated statistical model called logistic regression. With this model, different variables can be considered together to see if any of them might account for the apparent significance of another. With this model I was able to consider many different variables like age, belief in astrology, location of clinic, experience of depression, levels of anxiety and reproductive health problems together with astrology to see if any of them had an impact on any significant finding regarding astrology and treatment outcome.

The first exploratory study looked at 114 treatments and found that astrology, clinic location, and family history (reproductive health problems) all had significant associations with success and failure of outcome.

Between 2003 and 2005 I gathered new data from women patients attending to National Health Service (NHS) clinics and one private clinic for a replication study that was intended to test only the factors found to be significant in the first exploratory test. In the second study I examined 55 treatments and ran the model developed for the first study. This time, only astrology was significant with a 94 percent likelihood the result was not a chance finding.

ANS: What astrological methods did you use?

Dr. Harris: I developed the astrological model by referring to authors such as Ptolemy and William Lilly (17th century), who had described particular associations of astrology with times in a woman's life when she was likely to have children. Using these and other sources for information on ancient astro-fertility associations I divided the 114 treatments from my exploratory group into two treatment outcome groups: successes (resulting in the birth of a live baby), and fails (a live birth not achieved). I checked the astrology for each group using the women's birth charts and time of embryo transfers. To be determined was the absence or presence of astrological transits or secondary progressions that, traditionally, are believed to be present when children are born.

By carefully assessing the differences in each group I was able to build up a picture of a collection of astrological contacts that were significantly more likely to be present at embryo transfers for a successful outcome compared with embryo transfers that resulted in failure.

ANS: What are transits and secondary progressions?

Dr. Harris: An astrological birth chart (or natal chart) is a map of planetary positions in the sky at the time, date and place of birth for any individual. But the birth chart isn't static; it continually evolves or progresses over time.

As they orbit the sun, transiting planets form new stressful and/or helpful alignments with the planetary placements in an individual's birth chart. In the fertility study, the only significant transits observed involved transiting Jupiter aligned with or conjoined with either natal Sun or natal Jupiter in the birth chart.

To find secondary progressions astrologers advance planets in the natal chart using a day-for-a-year formula. Simply, in the progressed horoscope, planets in the natal chart are advanced the exact number of degrees they have actually traveled in a single day, either forwards or backwards. For example, to find out how far planets have symbolically progressed by age 30 the astrologer counts forward 30 days from the date of birth and casts a new chart for that day using the time and coordinates for the place of birth for the original birth chart.

Progressed planets can form new angular relationships with either natal or progressed planets in an individual's birth chart. In the fertility study a number of progressed alignments were significant when fertility treatment was carried out during the windows of time when these astrological progressions and/or transits were active. These included:

Progressed Sun and Venus making exact contact (a conjunction) within six months each side of the date when the contact became exact in the year or years being forecast.

Progressed Moon making exact contact with natal Venus within two weeks on each side of the date when the contact became exact in the year or years being forecast.

Progressed Jupiter making contact with natal Sun, Moon, Venus or Jupiter. Or Jupiter contacting the major angles (ascendant and midheaven) of the chart—all within three months on either side of the date when the contact became exact in the year or years being forecast.

Progressed ascendant or midheaven making exact contact with Jupiter and Venus within six months on each side of the date when the contact became exact in the year or years being forecast.

ANS: What can we take away from your fertility study?

Dr. Harris: The research did not directly confirm ancient writings on fertility indications in astrology. But it did clearly support the association of Venus and Jupiter with fertility and an increased likelihood of having children.

My original research increased the likelihood of a successful outcome when fertility treatment was timed to coincide with my researched astro-fertility windows by 10 percent when the birth time was known to within half an hour and 14 percent when the exact birth time was known. Continuing research with new data has enabled me to increase that percentage to 21 percent and 23 percent respectively.

ANS: What does the future hold?

Dr. Harris: I'm currently working on additional data and with alternative healthcare professionals with the objective of further improving the model and its effectiveness as a diagnostic tool. Importantly, the data I've continued to collect in my practice has supported the original study findings.

Testing Astrologers' Consciousness Levels

By Edward Snow

A study that examined consciousness development in professional astrologers has kicked a few holes in the notion that astrologers are a self-centered, superstitious lot with limited or faulty critical thinking skills.

"Critics of astrology often associate astrology and its practitioners with an unsophisticated, pre-modern world view. But this is not what we found," consciousness researcher and consulting astrologer Armand Diaz, PhD, reports.

Diaz is the author of *Integral Astrology, Understanding the Ancient Discipline in the Contemporary World,* and other books. He says models of consciousness development have become increasingly comprehensive and detailed in recent decades,and have been well supported with research. These models generally present the evolution of consciousness through a series of discreet, sequential stages that reflect both individual and collective development," he said.

In his independent research survey, Diaz focused on the general beliefs and values of 27 professional astrologers residing on three continents. Assessed was their level of agreement with seven sequential world views identified by developmental psychologist Jenny Wade.

Diaz says consciousness development takes place within individuals but also within societies and in historical epochs. In Wade's hierarchically-arranged system, each level of consciousness represents a more complex and inclusive perspective than the levels preceding it.

As a group, the astrologers had stronger identification with middle and upper ranges of consciousness and comparatively weak identification with the lower levels, Diaz said.

In Wade's system, naïve consciousness is associated with magical thinking, a high degree of preservation of sameness in both beliefs and activities, and an incomplete differentiation of the ego from one's clan or group. At the next level, egocentric consciousness, the newly formed independent ego recognizes its vulnerability and develops a "look-out-for-number-one mindset."

Conformist consciousness develops as the need to cooperate becomes apparent and belief in a universal way of believing and doing things develops. Achievement consciousness is associated with modern thinking and an unfailing belief in progress and personal independence.

At the next levels, affiliative (humanistic) consciousness reflects a desire to be inclusive and compassionate in addition to being successful. Integral (authentic) consciousness recognizes the value of the development process and essentially corresponds with the concept of self-actualization first described by psychologist Abraham Maslow.

Finally, transcendent consciousness focuses on overcoming the limitations of ego and reuniting with the fundamental source of consciousness.

Diaz says survey participants anonymously responded to 35 randomly presented statements—five each for the seven consciousness levels. On a seven point scale, participants were asked to grade how strongly they either agreed or disagreed with each statement.

"Statements identified with higher levels of consciousness should not appeal to those whose psychic center of gravity is at lower levels, and vice versa. If astrologers were truly acting from a primitive, superstitious, naïve or egocentric consciousness we would expect a higher level of identification with statements created to appeal to those at lower consciousness levels.

"For example, statements like it's generally unsafe to change the way we do things. Or, I'm on my own in competition with others around me," Diaz said.

As a group, astrologers participating in the survey strongly identified with the three highest levels of consciousness explored. Among other areas of agreement they strongly identified with the idea that "while people may hold different views and ideas, at a deep level all are fundamentally equal, he noted.

How Planetary Alignments Foreshadowed Arab Spring

By Edward Snow

That the Arab streets might be turning into a battleground for social justice at about this time was anticipated in the 2006 award-winning book *Cosmos and Psyche* by author, philosopher and social historian Richard Tarnas.

Tarnas is the founding director of the graduate program in philosophy, cosmology and consciousness at the California Institute of Integral Studies in San Francisco. He studied intellectual and cultural history and depth psychology at Harvard, earned a PhD in psychology from the Saybrook Institute in San Francisco, and worked and lived for more than 10 years at Esalen Institute in Big Sur, Calif., eventually serving as the institute's director of programs and education.

Tarnas is one of the few educators in the country doing serious social research involving planetary cycles. At Esalen with psychologist Stanislav Grof and others he began the qualitative study that eventually examined thousands of individual astrological charts.

"It was astonishing how the planetary alignments consistently and precisely correlated with human experience. The archetypal principles associated with the planets and the correlations uncovered were undeniable and uncanny in their subtlety and specificity," he said.

These patterns have permeated and shaped history over time, he suggests.

For example, at the time of its publication in 2006, *Cosmos and Psyche* offered a heads-up on an approaching alignment of the slow-moving planets Uranus and Pluto. The planets will remain "in aspect" through the year 2020.

Tarnas said the years 2007-20 would likely bring a new infusion of the cultural impulses and archetypal dynamics that emerged during the 1960s, which is the last time these planetary energies were in major alignment.

He points out that archetypal Uranus represents the principle of change, freedom, rebellion and revolution and is associated with unexpected phenomena of all kinds. Pluto, recently reduced by astronomers to dwarf planet status, is in fact a celestial heavyweight and the archetype for power itself.

"Pluto is the archetype of primordial energy and the universal life force that impels all evolution and transformation. It compels, empowers, overwhelms, transforms, destroys and resurrects. And, at its deepest level, it involves the mystery of death and rebirth," he explained.

Radical Social Change

Tarnas points out that characteristic themes observed for this cycle in past centuries include heightened impulses for radical social change and cultural creativity, accelerated technological and scientific advancement, the empowerment of progressive and reformist political movements, intensified feminist, civil rights and countercultural activity, an increased drive for freedom and autonomy at both the individual and collective level, and pressure towards radicalization in many spheres of action and ideas.

Also identified with the cycle is intensified ecological activism, large demographic shifts and the activation of mass energies and mass movements of various kinds.

"Generally speaking, Uranus-Pluto eras have tended to bring forth the catalyzing of powerful forces in many forms, the awakening of a will to power that can be both creative and destructive, and a tangible intensification and acceleration of human experience," he said.

In his book, Tarnas noted that while all of these specific themes have been strongly in evidence during past Uranus-Pluto alignments, precisely what would happen during the current 15-year cycle could not be known in advance. But it was apparent that a period of intensified striving for equality and self-sovereignty was on the immediate horizon, he noted.

Mercury Retrograde: A Tale of Two Elections

By Edward Snow

Astrologers say it rarely happens. But when the planet Mercury halts its forward progress on Election Day and starts moving backwards in the heavens it's Katy bar the door.

Astrologer Barbara Schermer says the Mercury retrograde phenomenon was clearly a factor on Election Day in 2000. In a tight race bedeviled by voting irregularities and delays, the U.S. Supreme Court stepped in to halt a recount of ballots in Florida that had been ordered earlier by jurists in the state.

The higher court's historic decision cleared the way for George W. Bush to win Florida's Electoral College delegates and pushed the candidate over the top in the national race. But the spectacle witnessed live on TV by the millions of Americans was hardly an inspiring portrait of democracy in action.

The indelible memory many have of this Election Day debacle is of election judges pouring over thousands of paper ballots abused by cranky voting machines. The judges were tasked with the insane job of deciphering voter intent by counting hanging "chads" that were insufficiently punched out on some Florida ballots, Schermer said.

Earlier this year, the astrological community warned that a similar celestial event was once again lining up for Election Day in 2012—for only the second time in modern history. Mercury was set to station (stop) on Election Day in the fiery sign of Sagittarius and begin its retrograde motion when the polls closed.

"There were concerns because we remembered what a mess the 2000 election turned out to be," she said.

Planet is the word ancient Greeks used for the "wandering stars" they observed contrarily moving at different speeds—and at times in different directions—through a firmament bedazzled by less adventurous fixed stars.

What the ancients didn't realize is that the retrograde motion they were observing was an astronomical illusion created by the vast and varying distances separating earth and its solar system neighbors. From an earthly perspective, observed direction changes appear to occur when the earth passes slower moving outer planets—or when faster moving inner planets appear to overtake the earth—as the earth elliptically orbits the sun.

Less easy to explain is why retrograde motion changes the way we experience archetypal planetary energies, Schermer says.

Messenger of the Gods...

To the ancients, fast-moving Mercury was the revered "Messenger of the Gods." Today the planet is intellectually identified with such things as mental acuity, flexibility and duality and is said to influence speech, writing, mathematical reckoning, information technologies and communications devices of all kinds.

When retrograde, Mercury is well suited for reflection, planning or strategizing. But under this influence human behavior becomes more quirky or mistake prone with problematic delays, uncertainty, false starts, miscommunication, miscalculations and the frustrating need to do things over.

Mercury's reputation as a trickster was largely earned during those times of the year when the planet is retrograde. Anything hastily built on an unstable platform is especially vulnerable, Schermer said.

On Election Day 2012 there were no hanging chads to count on Florida ballots or need to ask the highest court in the land to step up and decide a winner. Florida election officials did need an extra day to tally statewide results, but by then the race had already been decided in other battleground states in favor of the incumbent.

Voters did suffer the indignity of having to wait in long lines to reach polling booths in some states. But this development might as easily be attributed to deliberate efforts aimed at frustrating voter turnout and didn't seem to produce the desired result.

To everyone's surprise, the networks were able to call the race much sooner than expected. The losing campaign was so stunned by this unanticipated development it delayed conceding the election for more than 90 minutes after the outcome was obvious to everyone else.

Schermer says Mercury doesn't take sides in political elections. But on Election Day when the GOP rolled out an IT system that campaign organizers believed would give the challenger an electronic equalizer to combat President Obama's vaunted ground game, their best laid plans unraveled.

Called Orca, the system was named for the killer whale and was supposed to give the Romney campaign its own analytics on what was happening at polling places. Also, it was expected to aid get-out-the-vote efforts in key battle ground states.

The goal was to put a mobile application in the hands of 37,000 volunteers in swing states to help them track activity at the polls. The information provided was to be monitored and analyzed by more than 800 volunteers at campaign headquarters in Boston.

"Obviously, the candidate neglected to seek the advice of a competent astrologer. The system wasn't beta tested until election day—the worst possible timing for this sort of thing," Schermer said.

Thanks to a series of deployment blunders and network and system failures, Orca performed more like a floundering minnow. On the morning of the election 37,000 enthusiastic volunteers were left without communications or instructions for what to do.

"That's pure Mercury retrograde in my opinion," she added.

Part III

News and Views

Astrology Hiding Everywhere in Plain Sight

By Frank Piechoski

Is it lunacy to consider that the flu disaster chronology has anything to do with astrology—even on a Sunday?

In case you missed them, the above sentence contains six astrology-derived words in addition to the word astrology itself. Astrology itself can be considered a language of sorts. And just as languages borrow words back and forth, many languages borrow astrology terms and concepts.

The English language has many words whose etymology is derived from astrology—some are obvious, some are not. Some of the obvious ones are lunacy and lunatic—derived from Luna, the Moon. It is thought that the position and phase of the Moon affects people's mental states, thus the astrological etymology is rather direct.

Some other obvious astrology-derived words would be mercurial (Mercury), venereal (Venus), martial (Mars), jovial (Jupiter or Jove), saturnine (Saturn) and capricious (Capricorn).

The days of the week in many instances are also astrologically derived. Sunday (Sun), Monday (Moon), and Saturday (Saturn) are all readily apparent in English. Tuesday, Wednesday, Thursday, and Friday seem different—but only because English is from the Germanic family of languages and some of the days are named after the northern European equivalents of Mars (Tew), Mercury (Wotan), Jupiter (Thor), and Venus (Freya). The connection is a bit clearer in Romance languages.

Some words that find their roots in astrology are far less apparent. Consider this—*consider* is made up from the Latin *con* (meaning with) and *sideris* (starry; relating to stars; heavenly; star-like—the same root as sidereal). When one says they are going to consider something, one might just mean they are going to consult the astrology of the matter.

Similarly, the word *disaster* is a combined word with Latin roots—*dis* (bad) and *astrum* (star).

An even more obscure astrological origin is the word *flu*—or as it is fully known, influenza. It comes from the Italian through Medieval Latin—meaning that epidemics were thought to be under the influence of the stars. *Chronology* has its origin in Chronos, the Greek version of Saturn, the Lord of Time.

When someone wishes someone "Many Happy Returns" on their birthday, they are referring to Solar Returns—an astrological technique using the time once per year when the Sun returns to the position it occupied in the zodiac when the person was born.

Astrology permeates the English language to a degree not realized by the public—or even those who are well versed in astrology. Perhaps this will inspire some to examine even more words and terms—and there are many of them—for their astrological roots.

Is There an Asteroid with Your Name on It?

By Edward Snow

On the day former President Bill Clinton was born in Hope, Ark.,a harbinger of things to come was eerily projected in the alignment of several relatively large space rocks (asteroids) that were orbiting the sun more than 186 million miles away in the region of space known as the asteroid belt.

Asteroids come in various shapes and sizes and are believed to be the left-over remains from the dawn of our solar system. Astronomers have found, named or numbered thousands of these space rocks, most of which are observed circling the sun between the orbits of Jupiter and Mars. There also are the so- called near-earth asteroids that apparently have broken out of the asteroid belt and follow an erratic orbit that infrequently finds them whizzing by the earth—and occasionally running into it. In the past, scientist tell us that cataclysmic events like this have wiped out most living things on the planet.

But the dramatized images of huge boulders hurtling through space in a tight and menacing formation—a vision that comes to us from the science fiction industry—clearly presents the wrong idea. The asteroid belt itself is about 40 million miles wider than the space that accommodates the orbits of Mercury, Venus, the earth and Mars combined. And the asteroids buzzing around in all this space are relatively small, accounting all together for about the same amount of mass as the earth's Moon.

Some asteroids are small as a pebble. The largest, Ceres, is 600 miles in diameter and was recently elevated to dwarf planet status. But even this spherically-shaped object is relatively small by solar system standards—about 500 Ceres-size objects could fit inside the earth.

The asteroid belt objects closest to us are about 186 million miles from the sun with a solar orbit of three earth years, At the other extreme, the most distant asteroids are about 370 million miles from the sun and need twice as many earth years to orbit the sun. What this scale tells us: if we were sitting on an asteroid anywhere in the asteroid belt we'd probably need a telescope to see our nearest asteroid neighbor.

Technology to the Rescue

Ceres was first seen through an earth-bound telescope in 1801 and the discoveries of three smaller asteroids—Juno, Vesta and Pallas—followed in quick succession. With more sophisticated imaging technologies at their disposal—including orbiting telescopes and satellite flybys, astronomers today are discovering new asteroid belt objects on an almost daily basis.

It's up to the astronomers who find them to name, plot the orbits and document where their discoveries can be found in the heavens at any given time. At first, astronomers followed tradition and chose mythological names for their discoveries. However, when they became overwhelmed by the sheer numbers, astronomers began naming the space rocks for world leaders, historical characters, religious icons, celebrities and famous people of all kinds, including scientists, astronomers, mathematicians, physicists, historians, writers, actors, dancers and so forth.

In an article published on the Cosmic Patterns website, the late Jacob Schwarz, an astrologer, wrote that asteroids have also been named for loved ones, children and even family pets. There are asteroids named for countries, states, schools, colleges, mountains, rivers, plants, trees or whatever else inspired their discoverers at the time.

Names and tracking information for known asteroids are publicly recorded in official ephemerides. This is how we know that on the day President Clinton was born asteroids that included the names Monica, Paula and Williams were clumped together in a tight stellium or grouping that positional astronomers and astrologers call a conjunction. Although millions of miles may separate the asteroids in their solar orbits, on earth the trio appears to be occupying the same or nearly the same zodiacal degree on a two-dimensional astrological map.

Astrologers read conjunctions as powerful unifying or intensifying aspects that are made more purposeful when aligned with other celestial objects. For example, on President Clinton's birth date, the asteroids Hillary and Gingrich were also conjoined and aligned with Monica, Paula and Williams in a stressful 180-degree angular aspect astrologers call an opposition—for good reason. Invariably involved with oppositions are conflicts with others that must be resolved in some way.

A coincidence? The odds that asteroids conflicted in the President's birth map would so significantly match up with real life people and conflicts during the Clinton presidency are so long they defy calculation.

When dealing with asteroids, getting the names close is sometimes as good as it gets. When George W. Bush was elected president in 2000 and again in 2004 the transiting asteroid Busch conjoined the asteroid Washingtonia. When Germany, Italy and Japan formed the Axis nations before World War II, representative asteroids Germania, Italia and Nipponia were participating in mutually harmonious astrological aspects. All three were discovered and named decades before the war.

Timing is Critical

Gainesville, Fla., astrologer Michelle Gould says timing is critical when working with asteroids. In the Clinton example, the dynamic situation indicated in the President's birth chart didn't play out fully until years later when he was living in the White House.

Gould says she has observed a number of similar examples in the lives of ordinary people who come to her for astrological advice. When a young woman showed up for a consultation the astrologer noticed that the asteroid Buda was prominently positioned in her birth chart. Additionally, there were a number of other connections with the ancient religion and its shrines, including the strongly placed asteroids Tara, Lhasa and Mahakala, all tied to Tibetan Buddhism.

“At the time she came to my office the woman had just left her job to become a teacher of Green Tara practices, but had not been on this path for long. Had she come to me for a consultation a few years earlier her response to this information would most likely have been different. However, the way the timing worked, astrology was able to provide an enormous confirmation for her,” Gould said.

She says asteroids provide meaningful information in every birth chart she reads. Among the important connections in her own life, the asteroid named for evolutionary biologist Stephen Gould is prominently placed at the angle in her birth chart associated with marriage and partnerships. Her first husband’s first name was Stephen and her current husband’s last name is Stephenson. And she continues to use the surname (Gould) she was born with.

She thinks asteroid placements can provide a level of specificity not found elsewhere in the birth chart. In her work she finds them to be especially helpful as a story-telling tool that enables clients to access their own stories and better understand themselves. She attributes this approach to her mentor, astrologer and classicist Demetra George, who has written and taught extensively on the subject.

Is there an asteroid with your name on it? With thousands of asteroids orbiting the earth and astrologically connecting in various ways that’s a distinct possibility.

Time to Thank Your Lucky Stars?

By Edward Snow

It seems farfetched, but the horoscope column for a national U.S. consumer magazine once advised those born under the astrological sign of Gemini to take the night off and spend a restful evening at home on New Year's Eve—advice that almost certainly would have spoiled the fun for party-goers everywhere if heeded.

In an equally bizarre claim, a British newspaper told readers "it's time to count your lucky stars if you are a Gemini." The reason given: nearly one in 10 people included on a list of the 1,000 wealthiest individuals in Great Britain celebrated every birthday while the sun, as seen from earth, was transiting this particular astrological sign.

Astrologers universally acknowledge the importance of where the Sun resides in an individual's birth chart (horoscope). As British astrologer Frank Clifford puts it, "the Sun reveals our main life purpose, the core reasons behind why we're born and what we're in the process of becoming.

"The Sun shows how we picture and pursue our individual role in life's drama. And it shows the ways in which we ascribe meaning to life," he said.

However, predicting a universally awkward or anti-social New Year's Eve outcome for every Gemini on the planet is a stretch. And, says British research astrologer Robert Currey, placement of the sun in any of the 12 astrological signs at birth is not a reliable indicator of who is likely to be financially flush—and who is not.

Currey says the list of Britain's 1,000 wealthiest individuals is compiled annually by the *Sunday Times*. The story equating the sign of Gemini with accumulated wealth appeared in the *SUN* newspaper, which has the largest circulation of any national newspaper published in the UK.

A Bad Example

Currey thinks the study described in the news article "is a good example of bad astrology—and bad science,"

Gemini is the astrological sign identified with twins. The news article appeared under the heading: "A Gemini? You're Twin the Money."

Presumably, the way readers were supposed to interpret the catchy headline is that those born under the sign are somehow doubly blessed, or twice as likely to find themselves highly placed on a list of wealthy citizens. Only the facts presented in the news report don't support this conclusion, Currey says, adding:

"The fact that almost one in 10 on the 'rich list' were born under the sign of Gemini is not statistically significant. The odds that Gemini born are more likely to be counted among the wealthy are no better than chance.

"This is typical of the way astrology is sensationalized in the popular press and makes most astrologers and statisticians cringe. It's a shame the media fails to report the results from real research conducted by astrologers."

On his website Currey describes some of the problems that bedevil astrological studies that push findings based on Sun sign data alone.

Births, he explains, are not evenly spread throughout the year. In Western Europe the birth rate peaks in spring while in North America the rate is higher in both spring and fall.

What this means is that the various signs will either be over or under represented in research studies that fail to account for this fluctuation.

There's also the problem of people being born on the cusp between two signs. When this happens it's not possible to establish the individual's

Sun sign without knowing their time of birth. About one in 15 people fall in this category.

"What this says is that collecting an accurate representative sample of sun sign data for comparative research is hazardous and best compared with a control group," Currey said.

When analyzing birth charts, professional astrologers always look at where the sun is located in one of the 12 astrological signs. But they also check out the locations and the angular relationships formed between the Sun, Moon and planets.

"The astrological signatures in a birth chart for someone who has inherited vast wealth are very different from those in the chart of a self-made billionaire," he added.

Was Shakespeare a Fan of Astrology?

By Edward Snow

In the final act of Shakespeare's tragedy *Julius Caesar,* Mark Anthony describes Brutus, the man who came not to praise Caesar but to bury him, in these glowing terms:

"His life was gentle, and the elements so mixed in him that Nature might stand up and say to all the world, this was a man!"

This is rare praise indeed for an assassin. But Brutus had dispatched a megalomaniac (Caesar) whose ambitions threatened the cherished way citizens governed themselves in ancient Rome.

The Astrological Elements

Unlike most modern theatre-goers, those sitting in the Globe Theatre audience when the play was first performed 450 years ago would have been much more likely to pick up on the fact that the "elements" Anthony refers to are the astrological elements medieval astrologers considered when making judgments about the temperamental qualities inherent in man's nature. Most in the audience would have brought to the theatre at least a fundamental awareness of the concepts involved.

In her book, *Temperament, Astrology's Forgotten Key*, astrologer and classical scholar Dorian Gieseler Greenbaum, PhD, describes the system medieval astrologers used to categorize fellow travelers. It is based on the placement of planets in an individual's horoscope and identifies four basic temperament types: choleric, sanguine, melancholic and phlegmatic.

It's a bit more complicated than this, but very generally speaking the choleric type is fiery and energetic and the airy sanguine individual is the thinking, sociable and talkative type. The earthy melancholic is analytical, pragmatic and studious and the phlegmatic is contemplative, reserved and shy.

Positive and Negative Traits

There are both positive and negative character traits identified with each of the temperament types. And they rarely take time off.

Dr. Greenbaum makes the point that temperament is not the same as personality, although personality can incorporate parts of someone's temperament in its expression. Simply, personality is shaped by both internal and external factors whereas temperament is entirely innate.

"We are born with our temperaments, and while there may be overlays of one temperamental style or another during our lives, what we get is what we keep. A card-carrying phlegmatic does not suddenly become a raging choleric," she writes.

Early in the twentieth century psychiatrist Carl Jung described astrology as "the 5,000-year-old psychology of antiquity and the Middle Ages," elevating and placing the subject on a significantly higher level than his doubting Thomas professional contemporaries. Like Shakespeare before him, Jung was fascinated with how people managed and projected their uncompromising innate selves.

The ancient Greeks were first to write about the need to balance the elemental energies. Based on the cosmic alignments of planets at birth, one or more of the elements may dominate. Ideally, we get the sort of elemental balance the Greeks so admired—and Anthony believed Brutus typified.

Astrology in the hands of an artist like Shakespeare comes alive in characters at war with their own proclivities, or with the temperamental proclivities of others. The Bard was keenly aware of – and tended to exaggerate—how badly things might go. And he delighted in providing for his theatre audience glimpses of just how tricky—and sometimes outrageous—life's adventures can be.

Astrologer Frank Piechoski has a degree in theatre from the University of Wisconsin and has performed in several of Shakespeare's plays. He says the plays are full of rich imagery from many sources, including mythology, magic, astrology and science.

Clues in Shakespeare's Plays

In Shakespeare's day, both high-born and commoners employed astrologers but the practice was increasingly coming under attack from detractors on the science side. What Shakespeare thought about all this isn't clear, but Piechoski thinks there are clues to be found in his plays.

In King Lear, Edmund, the bastard son of a nobleman, rails against astrology in this way: "This is excellent foppery of the world that, when we are sick in fortune, often the surfeit of our own behavior, we make guilty of our disasters the sun, the moon, and the stars; as if we were villains on necessity; fools by heavenly compulsion; knaves, thieves and treacherers by spherical pre-dominance; drunkards, liars, and adulterers by an enforced obedience of planetary influence; and all that we are evil in, by a divine thrusting on. My father compounded with my mother under the Dragon's Tail, and my nativity was under Ursa Major, so that it follows I am rough and lecherous. Fut! I should have been that I am, had the maidenly star in the firmament twinkled on my bastardizing."

Piechoski says these bitter words are from the mouth of one of Shakespeare's most scheming and reviled villains, whose intrigues not only destroyed his own family but brought a kingdom to its knees. There are technical errors in Edmund's delivery astrologically hip theatre-goers would be expected to pick up on, he points out.

In contrast, from the comedy *All's Well That Ends Well,* one of the Bard's strongest and most capable heroines is a poster girl for astrology. Helena uses her mercurial wits and healing arts learned from her famous physician father to cure the King of France of an illness. In this era, healers used astrology to diagnose illness; her success in finding a cure earned from the grateful monarch a promise she could marry any eligible man in the kingdom she chose.

Shakespeare often called upon astrology to move along his plots and refine his characters. What follows is a conversation between Helena and the military officer who dragged her husband away to fight in the army of the Duke of Florence. That she had an exceptionally low opinion of Parolles, the officer, would be obvious to any astrologically astute theatregoers witnessing this hilarious scene:

Helena: Monsieur Parolles, you were born under a charitable star.

Parolles: Under Mars. I.

Helena: I especially think, under Mars.

Parolles: Why under Mars?

Helena: The wars hath so kept you under that you must needs be born under Mars.

Parolles: When he was predominant.

Helena: When he was retrograde, I think, rather.

Parolles: Why think you so?

Helena: You go so much backward when you fight.

Parolles: That's for advantage.

Helena: So is running away, when fear proposes the safety; but the composition that your valor and fear makes in you is a virtue of good wing, and I like the wear well.

By retrograde, Helena refers to the apparent backward motion of Mars as seen from Earth, which occurs approximately every two years. Shakespeare would expect his audience to pick up on the fact that retrograde Mars in the birth chart of a military man could prove to be a serious affliction. It might, for example, depict a warrior who is deceptive, cowardly or unable to take direct action when called upon, Piechoski explains.

As the play unfolds the full extent of Parolles' treachery, disloyalty and cowardice is exposed for all to see.

Piechoski says the playwright's command of astrological principles enhanced his understanding of the human condition and helped him to become the foremost writer in the English language. If you want to understand the plays the way his Elizabethan audiences did you'll need to brush up on your astrology.

How the Beatles Rocked with Astrology

By Edward Snow

What do you need when you start an ambitious business enterprise with Eastern spiritual leanings and a hippie sensibility?

If you're the fabulously wealthy Beatles pop rock singing group you open a trendy boutique on London's Baker Street and hire an in-house astrologer to advise on both personal and business-related timing issues.

The Beatles opened their first Apple Corp. business enterprise, the Apple Boutique, in December 1967. By this time, the rock group's coming-out party on the Ed Sullivan Show in New York City was in the rear view mirror, as was John Lennon's infamous "we're more famous than Jesus" remark, which incited denunciation and Beatles record bonfires in the U.S. and elsewhere.

In December 1967, the rock group's widely publicized visit to Rishikesh, India and the ashram of Transcendental Meditation™ founder Maharishi Mahesh Yogi was only months away. According to critics, this was a musically productive period and helped to solidify the group's image as counter-cultural icons.

The Apple Boutique was housed in an 18th century Georgian building just down the street from the fictitious 221B Baker Street address where

Sir Arthur Canon Doyle's famous fictional detective, Sherlock Holmes, purportedly lived and matched wits with evildoers from all walks of life. Originally, the Beatles had the building's exterior covered in a bright, swirling psychedelic mural created by The Fool, a Dutch art collective. But the flamboyant artwork was painted over after neighboring businesses and municipal officials complained.

The Beatles' Apple Corp. headquarters building and main recording studio opened on Savile Row in 1968. But the Baker Street property also housed two demo recording studios—upstairs and in the basement. On the main floor the boutique showcased clothing fashions and accessories for hip, upscale buyers of the sixties.

As Beatle Paul McCartney put it, the Apple shop was "a beautiful place where beautiful people can buy beautiful things."

According to an article posted on the Dangerous Mind website, the Beatles' in-house astrologer Caleb Ashburton-Dunning was assistant manager of the boutique and had an office in the building where he did daily horoscopes on demand for the group—and charts "for any special event or problem." However, the astrologer's arrangement with the rock group ended abruptly after he reportedly advised John Lennon that his fortunes would roll better if he dropped Yoko Ono and returned to wife Cynthia.

A Lifetime Flirtation with Astrology

Most likely, the Beatles' interest in astrological symbolism and timing didn't start with the Apple Boutique. For some members of the group, the flirtation with astrology was a lifetime passion that didn't end with Ashburton-Dunning's dismissal.

Astrological blogger Mary Barron points out that Beatle George Harrison was so into astrology he had his birth chart rectified to make certain he had the right time and date. He didn't.

Rectifying a birth chart is a sophisticated process that requires matching the progress of transiting planets and angles with actual events in an individual's life. Harrison was born near midnight and, before his chart was rectified, the date was recorded as February 25 at 12:05 am. However, Harrison's astrologer fixed the time a half-hour earlier on February 24 at 11:35 pm, and the rock star emerged as an individual whose life experiences were more in sync with his astrological map.

Barron explains that Harrison closely identified with his Pisces birth sign and rectification didn't change his sun sign. His deeply moving song, "Pisces Fish," appeared on *Brainwashed*—the album released posthumously in 2002 after its production was completed by his son. "It's a song deep with Piscean perspective," she noted.

"I'm living proof of all life's contradictions," Harrison sang. "One half's going where the other half's just been. I'm a Pisces fish and the river runs through my soul."

After rectification, the Moon in Harrison's chart remained in Scorpio, the sign known for probing the mysterious, for life-and-death concerns and for a "certain darkness," Harrison called himself a dark horse more often than he called himself a fish, Barron noted.

What most changed with rectification was the astrological sign rising on the eastern horizon at the time of Harrison's birth, which moved from Scorpio back into the late degrees of Libra.

"Libra adds a certain intellectual detachment, a love of beauty and a need for balance. Where the sun sign indicates the basic ego-sense of self, the moon represents one's emotional nature and the ascendant or rising sign one's dealings with the outer world. All come through with great strength in Harrison's theme song for his Sun sign," she said.

Astrologer Battles Back from Freak Accident

By Edward Snow

Life isn't always fair. In the movie classic *Some Like it Hot*, Sugar Kane Kowalczyk (the character played by Marilyn Monroe) bemoaned her fate in this way: "Story of my life. I always get the fuzzy end of the lollipop!"

The fuzzy end is that space where bad things happen to good people. Here we're keenly aware of inequities in the system and chafe at the apparent double standard that has some of us dealing with more challenging or catastrophic issues than others—with mixed results

Linda Furiate had been studying astrology for about a year when her ordeal began, triggered by an auto accident that left her reeling. After the crash she was diagnosed with cervical dystonia, a painful and incurable condition in which contracting neck muscles cause uncontrollable spasms. She wasn't able her to maintain her balance and experienced hideous jerky movements and abnormal posturing that caused friends and onlookers alike to recoil in horror. Her neck was twisted at an angle that made it impossible for her to look forward when she walked, so she found herself tripping over her feet and running into walls.

Things in her personal life fell apart. But Furiate wasn't ready for a pity party.

"I never asked why me? But I did ask why this?" she recalls.

All things considered, why this is the better question for an astrologer to ask. Furiate didn't see the accident coming but hindsight was revealing.

"Researching my chart revealed layer upon layer of evidence pertaining to how I was feeling physically, emotionally and psychologically. I noted the timing for the accident and saw that a transiting planetary configuration was in fact interacting with a stressful Mars—Saturn alignment in my natal chart. In a challenging way that related to my health and to the physical structure of my body and the muscle spasms I was experiencing," she said.

At the time of the accident Furiate's interest in astrology was enthusiastic but halting. However, seeing how the planetary patterns played out so dramatically in her own life changed all that.

"I was hooked," she said

Stressful Opposition

In analyzing her natal chart, Furiate focused on the stressful Mars-Saturn opposition that was "triggered" at the time of her accident. An opposition means the planets are roughly 180 degrees apart, usually but not necessarily in opposite astrological signs. When lined up in this fashion the Mars-Saturn opposition can indicate a crisis in action related to impulsiveness and the overweening need to control it.

Furiate began researching astrological medical books and found they confirmed Mars as the traditional "ruler" of the body's muscular system and Saturn its skeletal structure. Once she was able to rule out the possibility she was dealing with a brain or neurological disorder, she was able to develop a series of neck exercises, breathing exercises and posture improvement techniques that have helped her function symptom-free for extended periods of time.

Those demanding proof for astrological influences in human affairs might check out the compelling evidence in Furiate's on-going battle with cervical dystonia.

"Over the years I came to realize that when the planet Saturn changes signs and interacts with my natal Saturn or Sun there is a shift in how my body responds to my current treatment plan. There are times when I am mainly symptom-free and other times my neck is in such spasms—and my body so twisted—that it's hard to look at someone without moving my entire body towards them. Fortunately, I understand the rhythms of planetary motion and can adjust my life and treatment plan accordingly," she said.

Furiate completed a four-year training program with the International Academy of Astrologers (IAA) and has a growing list of clients. She also has picked up on the marketing career that was cruelly interrupted by her medical ordeal and works with both marketing and astrological clients from her home office in the Baltimore area.

Stressful Balancing Act

In her practice she balances gritty stoicism with a calming spiritual acceptance of the fact that life unfolds the way it does for a reason.

"Most of us tend to be blessed with multiple astrological aspects of either challenging or flowing energy. In my case, I find it is the challenging configurations that move me off the couch to do something about whatever the adverse situation might be. Everyone is born with troublesome issues to some degree. It's all a matter of how we choose to respond to life when something happens that throws us off course.

"Adversity provides us an opportunity to peek beneath the depths of our psychological make-up with the hope of finding revealing insights—or awakenings that may offer a newfound sense of wisdom or wholeness." She believes.

"When we lose any part of ourselves or fail to achieve something we planned on or hoped for a part of our identity may feel damaged or lost. It's always possible to get caught up in defining ourselves based on the roles we play—wife, boss, whatever. But these roles do not define our underlying purpose in life, they merely are the things we do. Our true purpose lies much deeper than that. When we haven't achieved something we've planned on we owe it to ourselves to reflect upon these desires and ask if they are truly what we want in the first place."

Furiate says an astrological reading may be helpful in determining why someone might long to be in a particular relationship only to find out that their behavior or attitude is pushing opportunity away. Or a reading may offer insights regarding the potential for obtaining something the client desires.

For example, she says one may dream of being a great motivational speaker and have hopes for sharing their insights and wisdom with the world. Only the placement of planets in their chart may suggest they are better suited to working behind the scenes. Astrological insights can help a client decide how to realistically pursue their desires.

"Philosophically, I believe each of us has taken on an earthly presence to learn, to grow and to experience love at its deepest level. The reason for intelligent life is to understand the purpose and complexities of the universe. Astrology is a great tool we can use to better define our existence and serve others," she said.

U.S. Capital Teeming with Astrological Symbols

By Edward Snow

When James A. Garfield, the 20th president of the United States, was felled by an assassin's bullet on September 19, 1880, the American composer and band director John Phillip Souza composed a dirge, *In Memoriam*.

And one of the most prestigious sculptors of the day, John Quincy Adams Ward, sculpted a statue of Garfield that was placed on an ornate pedestal on the road island to the southwest of the capital.

Perhaps only a few in the immense crowd gathered for the Garfield statute dedication noticed what appears to be an entire horoscope cast in bronze and depicting planets in astrological signs on the northwest side of the statue's plinth or base.

David Ovason, author of *The Secret Architecture of Our Nation's Capital*, believes this may be the only such astrological figure on any public statuary in the U.S. But, inexplicably, astrological symbolism is everywhere on display in public buildings and elsewhere in the nation's capital.

The city is teeming with zodiacs and zodiacal images. Many are in official buildings, including the Capitol Building itself where one would never expect to find such symbols of the spiritual world.

Teeming with Zodiacs

In Ovason's 1999 book he says, "There are 23 important zodiacs in the city and at least 1,000 zodiacal and planetary symbols."

Kenneth McGhee, an Arlington, Va., astrologer who lectures on the subject, suggests the number of important zodiacs in the city is higher. By his count there are 30 zodiacs with 12 of these located in the Library of Congress Building alone.

A tour of this building turns up a zodiac dome and zodiac clock in the main reading room. There's a floor zodiac in the Great Hall and zodiacs also are found in marble columns, in a granite arch, on the arm rail of the main staircase and in a hallway painting of Urania, who in mythology is the muse of astrology.

"There is even a zodiac in the wallpaper of a meeting room," he says.

The Library of Congress Building was completed in 1860. But there also are zodiacs in buildings completed much later in the 20th century, such as the ceiling zodiac found in the Senate Dirksen Building, completed in 1958, and a light fixture at the Ariel Rios Building, built in the 1930s.

McGhee says astrological zodiacs are visually prominent on armillary spheres located throughout the city in such diverse locations as the Air and Space museum, the Reston Town Center, Friendship Heights, Montrose Park in Georgetown and U.S. National Arboretum. These spherical sculptures are modeled after the instruments used by ancient astrologers to determine the location of celestial objects before telescopes were invented.

According to McGhee, the staid Federal Reserve Building and the Freer Art Gallery have zodiac light fixtures. And there are zodiacs on the Mellon Fountain and in the Hillwood Museum garden.

"But nothing is more bizarre than the arch zodiac above the alter at the Catholic Church's National Basilica on Michigan Avenue. Or the zodiac symbols embedded in an entry door at the National Academy of Sciences," he said.

So why do we find so much astrological symbolism in the nation's capital city today?

In his book, Ovason addresses the issue:

"The more I have explored the city and the more I have been touched by the many zodiacs it contains, the more I have marveled that so little research has been done into the arcane aspects of its design. One consequence of the scholarly silence is that the majority of my questions have remained unanswered," he writes.

Flirting with Astrology

But Ovason describes the Founding Fathers' flirtation with the esoteric ideals of the Freemason movement in the late 18th century. And he suggests this may somehow be connected with the proliferation of astrological symbols we find in the capital city today.

The city itself was planned by George Washington and was initially surveyed using stars as guides. The nation's first president was also leader of a Masonic Lodge, and Thomas Jefferson, Ben Franklin and many of the nation's other founding fathers were part of the Freemason movement.

In this era Masonic elders used astrology to time the laying of foundation or corner stones for every significant new structure rising in the district, including the White House and Capitol Building, he points out.

McGhee thinks the birth chart or horoscope he uses for the capital city provides some clues to the mystery.

"The city's birth chart has a lineup of planets (including the Sun) all clustered in that section of the horoscope astrologers identify with mysteries and the occult. Which fits with all the secret symbols found in the city today," he said.

Timing Critical For New Business Ventures

By Edward Snow

With about five of every 10 new startup businesses ending on the scrap heap within five years it's probably safe to assume that business failures happen for many different reasons. But it's not uncommon to hear those who fail say timing errors were largely to blame.

Financial astrologer Bill Meridian consistently ranks among the leading stock market timers in the country. He thinks the kinds of timing errors that often befall startup businesses—or occur when owners take private companies public—can usually be avoided.

Meridian has advised companies on incorporation dates, initial public offerings (IPOs) and other strategic timing issues. The founder of Cycles Research Ltd. has been forecasting markets with cycles for 40 years and is the author of *Planetary Stock Trading*, *Planetary Economic Forecasting* and *The Predictive Power of Eclipse Paths*.

It matters greatly how the planets, sun and moon are aligned at the time a business makes a critical corporate move. In the West, the number of businesses making this discovery appears to be growing dramatically in recent decades, he noted.

Meridian says timing errors made by businesses are relatively easy to spot. For example, astrologers were quick to point out where Facebook went so badly wrong when offering its shares to the public for the first time.

Facebook made its initial public stock offering on May 18. Three months later the shares were selling at half their original value.

According to Meridian, the company ignored the most obvious cyclical pattern in the heavens, the lunar cycle, and chose to bring the company public two days before a major solar eclipse. This was a major mistake.

"Events immediately before and after a solar eclipse are important. But events before an eclipse take on the added attribute of being unpredictable and fated.

"In the period prior to an eclipse we are in a shadow, not seeing the complete situation. If one is forced to make a decision or to take action prior to an eclipse, significant alterations in plans will be needed to reach the original objective," he said.

It's best to postpone a major corporate decision until the week following a major eclipse, he explained.

There were other problems for the social media behemoth. Astrologer Grace K. Morris says the chart set up for the exact time of the first trade indicates very difficult business challenges, most particularly in the area of financial accounting.

Morris writes the *Astro Economics Stock Market Newsletter*. The first trade chart for the Facebook IPO indicates the possibility of deceptive practices or at least confusion and misunderstanding, she says.

"There are indications the stock can still be a success but the company will need to work hard to overcome the unfortunate perceptions the public has as a result of its first public trade. The problem could have been avoided by picking a better time," she said.

Computer Genius Linked to Rare Planetary Alignment

By Edward Snow

Besides a genius for working with computers and making boatloads of money, many of the most influential people in the world of computing and information technology share another important connection.

In his latest book, *Outliers,* author Malcolm Gladwell reports that Bill Gates, the late Steve Jobs, Bill Joy, Eric Schmidt and Sir Tim Berners-Lee all were born during a critical 11-month period between November 1954 and October 1955.

Gates, of course, is founder and inventor of Microsoft and the Windows operating system. Jobs was Apple Computer's founder and developer of the Mac, iPod, iPhone and Pixar.

Joy is the co-founder of Sun Microsystems and, as the company's chief scientist, was involved in development of the UNIX and JAVA systems. Schmidt was Sun Microsystems' first software manager and is now the genius guiding daily operations as CEO of Google.

All London-born Sir Tim Berners-Lee did was invent the World Wide Web while at CERN, the European Particle Physics Lab in Geneva.

According to Gladwell, the list of information-age overachievers who entered the world during this critical time period doesn't end with this elite group. It also includes software innovators David Winer, who pioneered web blogs, RSS and podcasts; James Gosling, the inventor of Java software; Tim Bray, a former Director at Sun Microsystems now with the Android team at Google; and Ray Ozie, a software architect for Microsoft and the creator of Lotus notes.

Gladwell speculates that those born during this critical 11-month period benefited from a leap in technology at a key stage in their education. The rapid technological advances in the early 1970s ended the computer punch-card era and created "unprecedented access to computer mainframes and real-time computing while these individuals were still in their teens."

At least two members of the group, Gates and Joy, had an opportunity to acquire more than 10,000 hours of computer programming experience before beginning their careers, he said.

British astrologer Robert Currey, also born in 1955, taught himself to write astronomical and astrological software. Birth charts (horoscopes) produced using his popular Equinox program are marketed on the Internet and worldwide through a network of retail shops that includes The Astrology Shop in Covent Garden, London, and licensee shops in Dublin, Paris, Johannesburg, New York, Sydney and Portland, Oregon.

The Importance of Timing

Currey acknowledges the importance of fortuitous timing but says the technology "leap" that made computer punch-cards obsolete in the early 1970s was phased in over a number of years and doesn't explain the spike in the graph that occurred in 1955.

"On this basis, the distribution of computer geniuses by birth date should have increased exponentially throughout the 1950s and into the l960s," he said.

The astrologer believes a more compelling explanation involves a rare generational line-up of the planets Uranus and Neptune with Chiron, a comet-like body that is orbiting the sun between Saturn and Uranus. The configuration formed what astrologers call a T-square, and in every case was strongly aligned with personal planets in birth charts of the information age innovators.

The aspect started to consolidate in the heavens around 1952 and separated in mid-1958. However, throughout 1955, it was at its closest with a peak middle stage on June 11, just three days before World Wide Web inventor Berners-Lee was born.

Currey says Uranus is the planet most closely linked by astrologers to computers, information technology and intellectual breakthroughs. Neptune is connected with the process of merging the imagination and a world beyond existing boundaries.

Chiron was only discovered in 1977 but astrologers now associate it with the process of synthesis and integration. Its involvement in the stressful T-square aspect would have left the creative computer geniuses "with a feeling of dissatisfaction with the technology of the day and an awareness of the short-comings of their creations.

"They would feel painfully and self-critically conscious that it could be so much better no matter how much the world may praise them for their achievements," he said.

In addition to the computer wunderkinds, Currey said many inventive mathematicians, astrophysicists and chess masters were born under the challenging astrological aspect as well.

"The type of genius that manifests in any period of history is a reflection of the complex interaction between human, cultural and scientific evolution and the unfolding cycles of the universe. By connecting with the potential in their birth chart these individuals can embody and lead the zeitgeist—the spirit of the times," he said.

Was Jesus a Gemini?

By Edward Snow

Astrologers don't want to be collectively thought of as the Grinch who stole Christmas, but evidence from both Biblical and historical sources—and a star map of the ancient sky—suggest Jesus was born much earlier in the year, most likely in late May with the sun in the astrological sign of Gemini.

Astrologer Christine Arens says historians impressively argue against the December 25 date, when Christ's birth is traditionally celebrated by Christians around the world. A more likely date is May 29, 7 BC, she maintains.

According to History.com, the true date of Christ's birth wasn't known to early Christians. In the 4th Century AD, the Roman Catholic Church established the Christmas holidays in December near the winter solstice in order to blend in with pagan Saturnalia festivals observed in Rome and elsewhere in Europe.

Important Timing Clues

Historical records are sparse, but Arens says Scripture provides some important timing clues. For example, Scripture describes the appearance of angels heralding the birth of Jesus to shepherds who were watching their flocks by night.

“The sheep indigenous to this region have their mating season from October to December. With a five month gestation period, all of the new lambs would have been born by late May and the shepherds would be in the fields watching their flocks by night to make certain none of the newcomers went astray.

“What this gives us is a birth date for Jesus sometime in late spring.” she says, adding:

“The Roman historian Flavius Josephus writes about the illness and death of Herod, which occurred while a lunar eclipse was visible in Judea on March 13, 4 BC. Since the Bible tells us Herod was very much alive when Jesus was born His birth had to be prior to this date.”

An additional clue from the Bible: at the time of Christ’s birth Mary and Joseph had traveled to Bethlehem to register for their taxes. From ancient Roman records we know that three such calls for taxes were sent from Rome—in 28 BC, 8 BC and 14 AD.

“The 28 BC date is probably too early and the 14 AD date is obviously too late. Most likely, the 8 BC tax call is the one Scripture refers to,” Arens said.

Using modern computers astrologers can swiftly create a star map that shows the heavens exactly the way they would have looked to ancient astrologers more than 2000 years ago. From an astrological perspective, 8 BC was not an especially eventful year but the following year, 7 BC, was.

“Given the distances and communications challenges, it’s likely that most Jews would have registered for taxes in the year following the call, or in 7 BC when the heavens better explained the events unfolding,” she said.

Three Wise Men

Every Christian knows the story of the three Wise Men who followed a star to Christ’s birthplace. It’s likely these Wise Men, or Magi, were astrologer priests from the star cult of Zoroastrianism, a religious sect found in ancient Persia and Arabia that still exists today.

Arens believes the star the Magi followed was not an astronomical phenomenon, like a meteor shower, a comet or nova as none were recorded during this period. More likely, the Magi were anticipating an extremely rare coinciding of two naturally occurring astronomical cycles: a Jupiter-Saturn conjunction (which only occurs every 20 years) on the same day as a new Moon (Moon-Sun conjunction).

A conjunction occurs when planets line up in the same zodiacal degree. After observing a Jupiter-Saturn conjunction in December, 1603, astrologer Johannes Kepler proposed that the Christmas Star may actually have been a conjunction of these two planets. Arens agrees.

"When the planets involved in the conjunction are the two largest gas giants in the solar system they can light up the night sky spectacularly. This is what Kepler observed in 1603 and what ancient astrologers viewed in 7 BC," she points out.

Arens says archeological evidence confirms the ancient Magi astrologers were competent mathematicians and astronomers who understood the Saros cycle, which identifies the positions of new Moons and eclipses and how these positions regularly repeat themselves. The Magi astrologers would have realized that Jerusalem—and the town of Bethlehem nearby—was the only major urban area in the known world where both the sun and moon would be rising exactly together on the Eastern horizon.

This, she explains, is why the Magi traveled to Jerusalem.

"The ancient astrologers would have considered the coinciding of these two cycles to be an event of major significance. Two Roman emperors who claimed to be "divine" said they were born exactly at sunrise. A new moon sunrise birth would be even more significant.

"With the new Moon on Jerusalem's Eastern horizon it would be seen as bringing the power of the heavens to the physical world of the earth," she says.

This fixes the time for Christ's birth on May 29, 7 BC at 5:36 am with the Sun, Moon and the sign rising on the eastern horizon all at 4 degrees of Gemini. Jupiter and Saturn would be conjoined high up in the eastern sky (the Star in the "East") at 20 degrees of Pisces.

"Although maybe not the earthly king the Magi were reportedly looking for, with this combination Christ was born to be a great leader—a spiritual teacher and healer—who was destined to serve mankind," Arens concludes.

Famous Orchestral Suite Inspired by Astrology

By John Marchesella

When British composer Gustav Holst's orchestral suite, *The Planets,* was performed as an outdoor concert in New York's Lincoln Center the music was wedded with high-definition photographs, grainy videos and computer-generated images of the solar system. The seven movement orchestral suite was presented as: *The Planets—an HD Odyssey.*

It's unlikely that many in the audience were aware that the inspirational source for Holst was not the astronomical planets themselves but their astrological symbolism. Each movement is intended to convey ideas and emotions associated with the influence of the planets on the psyche, not the Roman deities.

Titles for each of the orchestral movements reflect astrological symbolism as well. For example, Mars is the Bringer of War, Venus the Bringer of Peace and Mercury is the Winged Messenger. Gas giant Jupiter is the Bringer of Jollity, Saturn is the Bringer of Old Age, Uranus is the Magician and Neptune the Mystic.

The idea for the work was suggested to Holst by Clifford Bax, who introduced him to astrology in Majorca in the spring of 1913. The composer became quite a devotee of the subject and liked to cast his friends' horoscopes for fun. He reportedly used Alan Leo's book, *What is a Horoscope?*, as a springboard for his own ideas.

As a work in progress, *The Planets* was originally scored as a piano duet except for Neptune, which was scored for a single organ. Apparently, Holst believed that the sound of the piano was too percussive for a world as mysterious and distant as Neptune. However, the suite did not become enormously popular until Holst scored it for a large orchestra. According to music critics, his use of orchestration was very imaginative and colorful, showing the influence of Arnold Schoenberg and other continental composers of the day rather than his English predecessors.

Curiously, although *The Planets* remains Holst's most popular work, the composer himself did not count it among his best creations and, late in life, complained that its popularity had completely surpassed his other works. He was, however, partial to his own favorite movement, Saturn—the Bringer of Old Age.

Astrologers might notice and be bemused by some of the astrological influences apparently at work here. Holst reportedly was born on September 21, 1874 at 4:24 pm in Cheltenham, UK. The astrological sign rising on the western horizon, his ascendant, was Aquarius. And the planet Saturn was conjoined (sitting atop) this angle of his birth chart (horoscope). The composer's disappointment with the work and affinity for the Saturn movement might prompt astrologers to say: "How Saturnian!"

Another notable point of synchronicity is *The Planets* was written between 1914 and 1916 when transiting Uranus moved over Holst's ascendant and into the first house of his horoscope. Among other things, the planet Uranus is associated with moments of heightened intuitive awareness and the first house with new beginnings.

Pluto was discovered in 1930 four years before Holst's death and was hailed by astronomers as the ninth planet. Holst, however, expressed no interest in writing a movement for the new planet. In 2000, the Halle Orchestra commissioned the English composer Colin Matthews, an authority on Holst, to write a new eighth movement, which he called Pluto, The Renewer. Matthews dedicated the movement to Imogen Holst, Gustav Holst's daughter.

Here's something else astrologers may find interesting: The musical theme from *The Planets'* fourth movement, Jupiter: the Bringer of Jollity, was merged with a well-known British poem. The first verse of the song was played at the Royal wedding of Charles and Diana and the second verse was sung at Diana's funeral. Astrologers point out that Jupiter is Diana's "ruling" planet, which means the planet, by virtue of its placement in her birth chart, was the most influential in her life.

What Does Regis Really Think About Astrology

By Edward Snow

Astrology," says the man who has spent more time in front of live television talk show audiences than anyone else on the planet "isn't for sissies."

In his book, *How I Got This Way*, Regis Philbin, an inveterate story-teller and master of "spontaneous conversation," describes a series of on-air meetings with the "remarkable" astrologer Sydney Omarr (his adjective).

Early in a broadcast career that spanned more than five decades, Philbin, who holds the Guinness World Record for most time spent in front of a television camera, was feeling incredibly blessed. With only a low-budget, live TV talk show in a secondary market (San Diego) to recommend him, he was asked to take over Steve Allen's nationally syndicated TV talk show, which was filmed in Hollywood at the time.

The first guest he booked on *The Regis Philbin Show* was Omarr, whose syndicated horoscope column was a staple in newspapers from coast to coast. The astrologer was asked to predict how successful the new show would be.

It was October, 1964. Omarr showed up and solemnly delivered the bad news.

"Sydney fixed a haunted gaze on me and said there's a fight going on right now behind the scenes as to what direction the show should go. He told me the show will fail. You won't make it," Philbin recounted.

In private after the show, Omarr told Philbin he was heading into the worst period of his life. "The earth will literally move under your feet," he warned.

Philbin worried about the dire forecast but was pleasantly surprised when his show was renewed after 13 weeks. So he invited Omarr back on the program to see if he was ready to change his mind about anything.

The astrologer was even more insistent. He told his host the show would be going off the air within 48 hours.

The end actually arrived 36 hours later when Westinghouse Broadcasting Company, the show's sponsor, lowered the boom.

The next few years for Philbin were as personally and professionally challenging as the astrologer had predicted they would be. Even the part about the earth moving under his feet.

Philbin owned a house on a hillside overlooking Universal City. At one point in 1968, it rained heavily for two straight weeks. On one of those rainy days half of his backyard slid into the canyon.

"City officials ordered the house evacuated. When I couldn't pay the bills to shore up the property, I lost the house entirely," he said.

Philbin had managed to land on his professional feet with a three-year stint as sidekick to Joey Bishop on the *Joey Bishop Show*. When this show was winding down after a disappointingly short run in 1969, he invited Omarr back to predict how things would go forward career-wise for Bishop and himself.

The outlook for Bishop was not especially up-beat. But the astrologer predicted Philbin was destined to become "a household name in America" and would have "great success."

When pressed for a timetable, Omarr said it wasn't going to happen right away. It would take another 20 years.

In his book, Philbin points out that Omarr made this prediction in December 1969. In September of 1988, his New York morning talk show, *Live with Regis Philbin and Kathie Lee Gifford*, was syndicated nationally and "we were well on our way to making that prediction come true," he said.

Show Host Interviewed by ANS

In an interview with the Astrology News Service (ANS), Philbin offered these insights:

ANS: What do you really think about astrology?

Regis: I was always fascinated by the subject for many years.

ANS: Did Omarr's gloomy forecast disturb you?

Regis: It sent a chill down my spine. I didn't believe it was going to be that bad, but it was.

ANS: What was the reaction of your show sponsors?

Regis: The sponsors and most of the people around me didn't believe in astrology in the first place.

ANS: Did you later learn that the show was already on life support when Omarr made the forecast?

Regis: Sydney was the first guest we had. His first forecast was an eye-raiser but when we got renewed for another 13 weeks I asked him to come back and that's when he became more definite. He said the death notice was 48 hours away. It came 36 hours later.

ANS: According to a report in the *N.Y. Times*, you thought bringing the astrologer onto the show would be a "good gag." Did you later change your mind about this?

Regis: I thought it was a daring and different way to start a new TV show.

ANS: Did you ask Omarr for advice of a personal nature?

Regis: Naturally I did and he repeated what he told me on the air. That like all good or bad things eventually it would come to an end.

ANS: Based on your first-hand experience, what would you say to someone who seriously asks for your opinion on whether astrologers might be on to something?

Regis: I was fortunate in those days to have Sydney Omarr join me. It makes me wish all astrologers could be as accurate.

ANS: What does the future hold for Regis Philbin?

Regis: Unfortunately Sydney is not around to answer that.

In his book, each chapter remembers a different celebrity guest and closes with a "What I Took Away from it All" summary of the experience. He closed the chapter devoted to his interviews with Omarr in this way:

"Astrology isn't for sissies. Those stars do seem to know things we don't—and maybe never should.

"Great things can happen much later than you might have hoped. But even then, great things are still great—and always worth appreciating—so don't give up."

Harry Potter Books Inspired by Astrology

By Edward Snow

Add author J.K. Rowling's name to the list of exceptional writers whose literary genius was inspired by astrological symbolism.

Rowling is author of the Harry Potter books, which have sold more than 400 million copies in several languages. In an article posted on his website, British astrologer Robert Currey points out that astrology "lurks in the background" in all the Harry Potter books.

"Astrology provides the structure and basis of the characterization for the Harry Potter series. One of the first clues is that the author provides every major character in the books with a birth date," he points out.

Like his creator J.K. Rowling, Harry was born on July 31. He is a Leo and personifies the heroic qualities of this Sun sign, Currey says.

"The Potter books cover Harry's heroic inner and outer battles to find his courage and destiny and to 'own' his own fame. Along this journey he undergoes a gradual process of individuation as he learns to accept his serpentine 'shadow' side."

Currey says Harry's friend Hermoine was born on September 19. Her "studious, brilliant, observant and critical nature is in line with her Virgo Sun sign."

Devoted sidekick Ron is poles apart. He was born on March 1.

"Ron's emotionally volatile and sensitive nature complies with Pisces. He feels insecure about his lack of recognition compared to his illustrious friend," Currey says.

Early on, few suspected Rowling's novels had anything to do with astrology. But Currey was among the first to publicly comment on this possibility.

The sale of a rare unpublished work by Rowling on the BBC TV series Antiques Roadshow a few years later confirmed his suspicions.

The rare "book" offered for sale on the TV program was an illustrated 12 page type-written natal analysis (horoscope reading) Rowling prepared for the son of a woman she befriended as the pair awaited the births of their first children. At the time, astrologer Rowling was otherwise preoccupied writing her first novel, *Harry Potter and the Philosopher's Stone,* which published in 1997.

"While J.K. Rowling may not be an accomplished astrological consultant it is clear that she has a deep understanding of astrology and mythology well beyond her studies of the classics at Exeter University. And she has used this knowledge to great effect in her novels," Currey believes.

For example, in the Harry Potter books the protagonist is taught by Firenze, a Centaur who foretells the future using his observations of the heavens. According to an article in the *Sunday Mirror* newspaper Rowling said the Firenze character was inspired by real-life astrologer Steve Eddy, co-author of *The New Astrology: The Art and Science of the Stars* with Dr. Nicholas Campion.

Teacher Knows Best?

Eddy was Rowling's English teacher when she was 11 years old at Wyedean comprehensive school in Sudbury, Gloucestershire. At the time she wasn't using initials to mask her given names.

Eddy was quoted in the *Sunday Mirror* article:

"Joanne's work always showed impressive imagination and in class she was always bright and enthusiastic, much in the way of Hermione in the Potter books. But when it came to her stories, they were always about elves, pixies or fairies.

"I was constantly telling her that she was at an age where she should be writing about grittier, more real-life things. Thank goodness she never heeded my advice."

Currey says anyone familiar with J. K. Rowling's style of writing will know that every detail has meaning. "She writes about a magical Neoplatonic world, not a random, meaningless, muggle universe."

Astrologers will identify with the four school houses at Hogwarts because their qualities seem remarkably like the four astrological elements: fire, air, earth and water.

Also, members of the Black family are all named for fixed stars or constellations.

"Harry's godfather Sirius Black is able to transform into a dog (his animagus).

Ancient Egyptians called Sirius the Dog Star after their god Osiris, whose head in pictograms resembled that of a dog."

But Rowling's subtle, nuanced references to astrological symbolism will not be apparent to most readers.

"Perhaps wisely, the author didn't hook her wagon to stargazing from the start as there is plenty of prejudice and ignorance that could have adversely affected sales of her outstanding books," Currey said.

Nevertheless, he thinks Rowling joins the ranks of Chaucer, Shakespeare, Margaret Mitchell (*Gone with the Wind*) and C.S. Lewis (*Narnia*) "in an illustrious group of writers who were inspired by astrology."

St. Peter's Basilica an Architectural Triumph

By Edward Snow

When the Holy Father and other 16th century leaders of the Roman Catholic Church sat down to plan construction of St. Peter's Basilica in Rome the first person they reached out to was not Michelangelo or any of the other distinguished architects or designers who worked on the project.

"St. Peter's Basilica is considered by many to be an enduring affirmation of a centuries old theology and a grand example of Renaissance architecture. Astrology may not come to mind immediately for the millions of visitors who take in the spectacle of the awe-inspiring building each year, but construction of the church was in fact begun on a certain date and at a precise time chosen for its astrological significance," says Mary Quinlan-McGrath, a professor of art history at Northern Illinois University (NIU) and author of *Influences: Art, Optics and Astrology in the Italian Renaissance*.

Quinlan-McGrath writes that before any work began the astrologers of Pope Julius II established that the horoscope for the start-up of construction (April 18, 1506 at 10 a.m.) correlated with both the horoscope for the presumed birth of the world and the birth horoscope of Christ.

"The locations on the horoscope chart of the Sun, Venus and Mercury indicated benevolence while that of Saturn and Mars suggested power and longevity. Jupiter's location was propitious as well, promising wealth," she observed.

Quinlan-McGrath says Pope Julius II and his Renaissance architects believed that "the concordance of the heavens and the radiation emanating from the cosmos provided protection for the building at the time of its founding and, in turn, the building would continue to radiate these powers upon the people associated with it over the centuries."

In the current era, modern astrologers aren't likely to go along with the date their medieval counterparts used for the birth of the world. And the date divined for Christ's birth is suspect as well.

However, despite these factual stingers, most contemporary astrologers would probably agree that Vatican astrologers did an excellent job of finding an enduring electional chart for the start of construction.

Using modern computers, astrologers can swiftly pull up a birth chart that displays the heavens precisely as they looked on April 18, 1506 at 10 am in Rome. The planetary alignments on that day were exceptionally harmonious—with one notable exception.

Medieval astrologers used the Sun, Moon and visible planets in their calculations. On the Basilica's electional chart the major stressful aspect is a hard, right-angle alignment between the Sun and Saturn, with Saturn dominantly controlling that space on the horoscope wheel astrologers look to for insights on financial matters.

Aspect Proves Challenging

Astrologers in any era would notice that the angular relationship between the Sun and the planet associated with hardship and delays (Saturn) would be challenging. And, in fact, the project was plagued by more than a century of financial woes and construction delays, Quinlan-McGrath points out.

Presumably, Vatican astrologers were mindful of the economic stressors the project was fated to face, but had supreme faith in the positive, long-range outcome promised by the electional map.

In her book, Quinlan-McGrath examines the astrological context of the founding of Saint Peter's as well as the creation of other works of art and architecture in Rome, such as the Stanza della Segnatura in the Vatican Palace and the lavish Villa Farnesina of Agostino Chigi, an extremely wealthy banker.

She notes that astrological thought permeated the Italian Renaissance. Scientists used mathematical measurements to chart the heavens and theologians and philosophers harmonized religious doctrine with astrological readings, making Saint Peter's a product of its time.

"The belief that celestial forces could operate through works of art and architecture was not obscure or magical but in harmony with the philosophical, religious and scientific beliefs of the fifteenth and sixteenth centuries," she explains.

How Astrologers Aided Info Industry Giants

By Edward Snow

When you pick up your smart phone and scroll through any app that allows you to select your time zone you're holding a piece of technology that was made possible, in part, by the research of astrologers.

Yes, you read that right: astrologers.

Astrologer Donna Woodwell says knowing the precise time in a given location is a key ingredient in casting an astrological birth chart. For most of history, timekeeping has been a local affair—when the Sun was directly overhead it was "noon" and clocks were set accordingly.

However, with the advent of mass transit and mass communication came the need to standardize timekeeping. An international convention met in 1884 to set the international dateline and establish 24 global time zones.

Since then, how individual countries and cities have related to this global timekeeping tapestry has been an ever-evolving system. Consider Daylight Saving Time, how regions on the border of time zones shift their temporal allegiance, adding leap seconds and other changes and a picture of the complexity of the question "What time is it?" emerges, she noted.

"To keep up with these changes, astrologers have done what they have always done—they keep records. Over the decades, hundreds of astrologers have shared their data with one another," she said.

In the pre-Internet days, astrologers contributed to periodicals like the *Mercury Hour*, to the collection efforts of individual astrologers such as Doris Chase Doane, or through astrological organizations like the American Federations of Astrologers. Astrologers used these sources as references for determining birth time when calculating charts by hand, Woodwell points out.

Then in 1978, Neil Michelsen's company ACS Publications released *The American Atlas* (followed in 1985 by the International Atlas.) Astrological researcher and programmer Thomas G. Shanks combined the materials from earlier astrologers with data from national railway schedules and other public sources, as well as his educated guesswork, to create the most comprehensive single source for time zone information available at the time.

Woodwell notes that with the advent of the information age, computer networks rapidly grew in complexity. Programmers of computer operating systems also recognized the need to have access to accurate information on time zone changes for desktop computers, transportation systems, banks, commerce and more.

In the late 1980s a group of programmers and researchers, including Arthur David Olson and Paul Eggert, began to collaborate to create a standardized time zone database optimized for the needs of the information age. Although their time zone database (also known as the tz database) has an original database structure and a large number of volunteers who update and improve the database, when it was first established one of its sources for time zone data were the Thomas Shanks astrological atlases published by ACS.

"In other words, data collected over decades by astrologers in order to produce accurate birth charts became a building block of time zone calculations used by modern information giants such as IBM, Apple, Google and others. Not since the days when astrological ephemerides of planetary positions were used by scientists to demonstrate that the Earth moves around the Sun has data collected by astrologers played such a role in the evolution of technology," she said.

Some Thoughts on Fooling Around with Fate

By John Townley

Every birthday you get a celestial present you may not know about …

For all the positive free-will spin modern astrologers have put on astrology, it's still a bit like the weather—everyone's always talking about it, but nobody ever does anything about it. The planets deal their ever-changing cards, and we play the hand we've been dealt as best we can.

Of course, as with the weather, we can be smart enough to know to go inside when it rains, and that smacks a bit of free will, and it's what most people use astrology for—to know when to batten down the hatches or when it's a good day for the beach. But astrologically, we can do even more: we can actually go to where it isn't raining on our lives—or at least change the form of precipitation and where it's likely to hit us. To a limited extent, we can actually derail destiny, fool around with fate—if, indeed, astrology has any more effect on either than do common and often critical daily choices.

That can be done, so far, in two different ways.

The Solar Return Chart

Every birthday, you get a celestial present that you may not know about, unless you're an astrologer. And even if you are, you may not take sufficient advantage of it. It's called a solar return—a horoscope for the instant the Sun returns to the exact place it was at the precise time of your birth. It happens every year or within a day of your birthday, so it's a birthday present that both tells you a lot about the coming year and, if you handle it properly, gives you some extra control over how that year turns out.

The easiest, but most temporary, way to control outcomes is to choose well where we spend our solar (and to a lesser extent our lunar) returns. If your next solar return birthday chart has a nasty afflicter squatting right on the Ascendant (the Western horizon) no problem. Just take a trip and spend your birthday a time zone or two East of where you'd normally be, and that bad boy is tucked safely away in the hidden twelfth house, where it can do you less tangible harm for the year. Or, if it looks like your solar return Sun or Moon is going be trapped in the twelfth, a time zone or two of Western travel will roll it right up front into the first house, where it can really work for you all year.

It's a good excuse for birthday vacation travel. And, If you really get into it, you can investigate all sorts of places that amazingly maximize benefics and minimize malefics for the year. I know so many astrologers and their clients who enthuse about the results—although you can't compare what actually might have happened with what did in any year, whether you travel or not. But the tales of positive shifts, and their details, can be pretty compelling.

Since I've traveled a great deal for my solar returns, I've got a lot to tell, probably the most convincing about when I couldn't make the needed trip because of happenstances and walked eyes wide open into a disastrous year involving events totally not of my own making but which night have been easily avoided with a plane trip. Like the year of a horrible twelfth house Sun with Saturn rising, Moon in the sixth afflicted by Neptune. Looked like illness for sure. As the solar return paints the picture of the new you for the year, which meant physical difficulty (Saturn on the ascendant), the life-giving Sun tucked away in a dark corner (the twelfth house) and confused feelings (Moon afflicted by Neptune, in the house of health). Not the picture of me I wanted for the year.

On a limited budget, a flight to a couple of small selected towns in the South would just beat it out, putting a more robust Sun right on my ascendant. But tropical storm Fay came along at the last minute and all possible flights were canceled. I was stuck in New York with my dreadful return. My subsequent year was spent in and out of hospitals, drawn with pain, thanks to repeatedly misdiagnosed kidney stones (that Neptune-Moon sixth house affliction). Was this cause and effect, or just cosmic synchronicity? A bit of both, I expect…the illness was on its way and that, along with Fay, probably conspired with the cosmos at large to shoot down my travel plans. You can't dodge the bullet with your name on it. And although they say if you are born to hang you'll never drown, if you're born to drown all it takes is a puddle.

On the upside, every place I've successfully visited to get a better solar return has filled me with joy and mystery, even when (perhaps particularly when) it's an out of the way place I wouldn't think to go except for its momentarily convenient longitude and latitude. That's a feeling I share with many of my clients who regularly travel to get a better year. A typical comment from a client who recently travelled from California to Niagara Falls:

"Everything about the journey had a mystical quality to it. As if, somehow, I found a portal to another dimension. And really my only regret is not staying longer."

Often my feelings exactly, and the results of being in an unusual place at an unusual time can provide an experimental twist that may not entirely surface until years later, altering your life and taking your breath away when it does. Under the circumstances, it can't hurt and is a great excuse to take a break and get out of town!

Relocation: Go There, Stay There

Of course, if going for a visit is so great, why not live there? That's the other way you can actively change otherwise-ineluctable effects of the planets. A quick look at an AstroCartoGraphy chart showing where around the world your planets would be rising or culminating will tell the tale. You'll be energized in spots where Mars, Jupiter, or the Sun are angular, slowed down by places where Saturn is the same. If you've traveled much, the map is a revelation, explaining a lot about why certain things tend to happen to you en you go certain places. It's not a total replacement for your natal chart, but it can really put a spin on what's available for you in different places.

Astrologers check out midpoints, which are points that equally divide (in degrees) the distance between transiting planets. With my Venus/Mars midpoint going straight over New York City, the Big Apple is just too sexy to escape from, for me, though for others it can spell misery. With Mars/Uranus culminating (directly overhead) in Poland, that country sets me on fire with instant fame, but also puts me in more danger than I'd like, with some close calls I wouldn't like to repeat. But with mellow Mercury rising over Southern England I dream of spending my latter days near Glastonbury writing and letting the amazing ambience of the Old Straight Track suffuse my bones.

Free Will A Possibility

Returns and relocations are for the moment the only ways you can take the celestial bull by the horns and wrestle it to where you want to go, simply by changing the houses (locations on the chart wheel) where planets occur. You can't change the relations of the planets to each other—well, not so far. In a few generations, we will no longer have these restrictions. When you can go to the Moon (as our children or grandchildren will) you'll remove the Moon itself in any chart you look at and replace it with a transiting Earth exactly opposite to its former position. Go further afield, once we've teraformed Mars (or at least learned how to make it a bit more friendly), and the entire set of aspects between all of the inner and middle planets will be totally rearranged as long as you are there. And so will the tropical signs themselves as Mar's tilt and orbit creates a whole set of Zodiacal signs and seasons totally different from ours here on earth. You will be able to change everything—houses, signs and aspects—completely according to where you decide to travel.

That travel broadens one's outlook is more than just a philosophical observation—it's at the heart of exercising free will in an astrological context. The farther you go, the further you can go…

Will it ultimately free you to do anything you want? Probably not. Not anymore than I could escape the collusion of tropical storm Fay and my kidney stones. You can cut yourself a whole lot more slack by giving it your best shot than you ever could by simply staying put and accepting what comes.

The Astrologer Did it: A New Kind of Mystery

By Armand Diaz, PhD.

There's a new mystery subgenre that's growing in popularity, what we might call *astro-detective* fiction. In a number of recent books, the protagonist uses astrology to help solve mysteries. Perhaps surprisingly, the books are not coming from established authors of detective fiction, but from some very well established and respected astrologers. Steven Forrest, Alan Annand, and Joyce Mason are three well-known astrologers who have taken the leap into the realm of astro-detective fiction, and the results are impressive.

Actually, the subgenre isn't really new, but lately titles are popping up more and more frequently. Steven Forrest got the ball rolling with *Stalking Anubis* back in 2002, although determined readers, themselves acting a bit like detectives, can find titles going back to the 1940s.

Readers unfamiliar with astrology have nothing to worry about with astro-detective fiction, as the actual astrology is never demanding in these books. Mystery fans are used to being led through technical territory anyway—you don't really need to know much about forensic science, the chemistry of poisons, and so on, in order to appreciate that the detective *does* know about those things. Readers with some familiarity with astrology will be able to follow the way the detective uses the information, but novices will not feel left out.

After all, we have to remember for the most part detective fiction is as much about the personality of the detective as it is about the logic of problem solving. Even readers who try to follow along closely will often find that key information has been withheld or reinterpreted in ways that were bound to surprise. No, it isn't logic but the detective's personality that makes the book worth reading, and fictional detectives tend to have very quirky personalities.

From Sherlock Holmes and Nero Wolfe to Lieutenant Colombo and Monk, we are enthralled by the unique genius of the detectives—and who makes for a quirky genius better than an astrologer?

Personalities differ among detectives. Sherlock Holmes is an aloof genius, Sam Spade is a hardboiled tough guy. In astro-detective fiction, we also find a great deal of variation. One of Alan Annand's creations, Axel Crowe, is a near-ascetic Vedic astrologer who easily exercises self-control as he sleeps in the same room as his potential love interest in *Scorpio Rising*. On the other hand, Joyce Mason's heroine in *The Crystal Ball* is tougher and more down-to-earth, as West Coast detectives seem to be. Actually, Mason's character, Micki Michaels, isn't really a detective so much as an astrologer drawn into a mystery, a typical device in astro-detective fiction.

What makes mystery such an enduring genre? It seems to me that we love the mixture of focus and urgency. We know what needs to be done, and that it needs to be done soon. The question is: *how* is it going to be done? For that, we need to rely on an expert, someone with a unique set of skills, a hunk of determination, and a touch of genius.

Readers who want a good mystery will find that astro-detective novels fit the bill and make for an interesting, fun read. I've given you some leads and dropped a few clues… now it's up to you.

Making the Case for Financial Astrology

By Edward Snow

As early as 1994, financial astrologer Ray Merriman began persistently warning anyone within earshot that a huge stock market decline and financial crisis would upset the global economic applecart in 2008. While there were other astrological factors to consider, Merriman says his prediction was largely based on the angular relationship between transiting Saturn and Uranus—a 180-degree opposition aspect that would be forming in the heavens at this time.

Financial astrologers view Saturn's role as defender of the status quo. Among other things, antsy Uranus represents the irresistible urge to break away and try something new. In the past, when this particular celestial standoff has occurred at the same time planet Pluto is transiting in one of what astrologer's call the cardinal signs (Aries, Libra, Cancer and Capricorn), the event has coincided with troubling news for the banking and investment communities. Merriman started calling the pending aspect the "Cardinal Climax," a phrase now commonly used by a growing legion of financial astrologers around the globe to describe this event.

Merriman admits he worried that "hard" or challenging aspects between slow-moving Saturn, Uranus and Pluto would be forming again in 2010 and 2014. The expectation was that more bad news might be on the way, but the largest market intervention in world history by central bank policymakers nullified this possibility. The Fed lowered interest rates and later began buying Treasuries and mortgage-backed securities in an effort to stimulate spending and economic growth. With help like this the stock market was able to soar to record highs.

"When you have more money buying securities than selling them, well, that makes the price go up. Which, of course, was the Fed's purpose," he noted.

The author of nearly 50 books, Merriman writes the monthly Merriman Market Analyst newsletter (MMA Cycles) and both a weekly and daily forecast for more active traders. His life work has been divided about evenly between his role as a professional astrologer and accomplishments achieved in the more pragmatic world of business and investments. He appears equally at home in either milieu.

Merriman is a commodity trading advisor (CTA) and passed both the Series 3 (commodities) and Series 7 (securities) exams while working as an analyst at E.F. Hutton in the 1980s. He is a member of the National Futures Association (NFA) and served as an arbitrator in disputes for several years. In his final Wall Street job he was accounts vice president of retail commodities futures at Paine Webber. Currently, he heads the Merriman Market Timing Academy (MMTA), a global enterprise that is training traders to integrate astrology with other market-timing tools.

On the astrology side, Merriman passed the American Federation of Astrologers (AFA) professional astrology exam in 1972. His degree in psychology and subsequent graduate studies at Michigan State and Oakland University helped prepare him for a career as a consulting astrologer. He describes serving as President of the International Society for Astrological Research (ISAR) between 1994 and 2000—and again between 2002 and 2008—as high points in his career.

In an interview with ANS he provided these insights:

ANS: How did it all get started for you?

Merriman: I started studying astrology in 1966 and passed the American Federation of Astrologers (AFA) professional astrology exam in 1972. By 1977, I had written two well-received astrology books: *Evolutionary*

Astrology: The Journey of the Soul Through the Horoscope, and *The Solar Return Book of Prediction.* The solar return book has become a standard in astrology with about 20 printings since it was first introduced. Only 1,440 copies of *Evolutionary Astrology* were published and the book sold out in three years. It was done in calligraphy—a beautiful book that will never be reprinted but sometimes is available on Amazon.com.

ANS: What are the most important things people should know about you?

Merriman: Perhaps it's that I love to write—every day. I enjoy waking up and either researching something that interests me or writing about it in a way others can understand. The financial markets -and life itself—are puzzles for me with parts scattered all around. The challenge is to find the pieces that fit together.

ANS: What do you regard as your most important achievements?

Merriman: Professionally, I would say the authorship of nearly 50 books involving astrology—from the first books in 1977 through the completion of nine financial market-timing books in 2010. The financial series started with *The Gold Book: Geocosmic Correlations to Gold Price Cycle* in 1982, and culminated with a five- volume series entitled *The Ultimate Book of Stock Market Timing.* All together books in this series total about 1,600 pages. I believe they helped make a difference by bringing astrology out from the belief that it is purely a form of entertainment or superstition to the idea that there is something of great value here for society.

As ISAR President I worked with a great group of people that challenged each other to build something big and great for astrology. During my terms ISAR grew from probably the smallest national/international astrology organizations to one of the largest and most active. Highlights included the creation of a certification program, a consulting skills program and a competency exam. The organization initiated the ISAR online e-zine, which did wonders in bringing the membership together. And we held several highly successful international conferences, each built around topics of interest to the worldwide astrology community.

ANS: At astrology conferences the number of attendees participating in programs dealing with financial astrology appears to have mushroomed in recent years. What's going on?

Merriman: It works! Nothing is as consistently accurate in identifying reversal times in financial markets as astrology. I think a few of us as financial astrologers have been able to convey that awareness to the trading community. Astrology appeals to traders because it provides that extra edge all traders seek. They want to learn more, and the way to do that is by attending conferences or workshops on the subject.

To give you an idea… I was amazed by how many people (40) signed up for my new two-year Merriman Market Timing Academy program that launched in April 2013, because the program is not cheap ($20,000). Both traders and other astrologers joined the initial program because they wanted to learn how financial astrology works.

ANS: When did you decide to focus full time on financial astrology?

Merriman: I started writing the MMA Cycles report as a purely gold and Silver report in 1981. I had 35 subscribers when I released *The Gold Book* in November 1982. Right after it came out I was invited to fly to Los Angeles for an interview with Bill Griffith and Leibe Geft of the Financial News Network (FNN). I was their guest for an hour-long interview the next day on Money Talk. When I returned to my office the next week I had over 1,000 letters and 350 new subscribers. I had to quit my day job as an astrological consultant and, over the next six months, transitioned into a full time financial astrologer and market letter writer.

The MMA Cycles newsletter was expanded to cover first the stock market and then Treasuries, currencies, grains and crude oil—all by popular demand. I became a hot commodity myself and was a frequent guest contributor on the FNN network and was quoted on investment topics in major business and financial publications, like *Fortune* and *Forbes*.

ANS: So the message is getting across?

Merriman: Traders love astrology and are the lifeblood of my company. Every year I do an annual forecast book that is translated into several different languages and sells about 7,500 copies. Subscribers for daily, weekly and monthly reports vary between 800 and 1,000 at any given time. And I've been invited to speak to large groups of bankers and international traders in Japan, London, Switzerland and other countries around the world.

Astrology Making Progress in Britain's House of Commons

By Edward Snow

The world may not be ready for this, but astrology has a pulse in Britain's House of Commons where Conservative MP David Tredinnick fearlessly serves on both the health committee and the science and technology committee as an open advocate for the ancient art.

He admits to casting the occasional astrological chart for colleagues in Parliament, and recently told BBC News he's not afraid of the ridicule and abuse that comes his way.

"There is no logic in attacking something that has a proven track record," he maintains.

Mr. Tredinnick says he studied the Indian astrological system lahiri and the way it was used by that country's government. And he recalled how Chris Patten, Britain's last governor of Hong Kong, had an official astrologer.

The MP said he consulted with the governor's Hong Kong astrologer while on a parliamentary delegation there.

Mr. Tredinnick recently expounded upon his beliefs at the Glastonbury Festival, where he shared the stage with *Daily Mail* astrologer Jonathan

Cainer. At this event, he said he was invited to serve on the health committee in the House of Commons because of his radical agenda on complementary medicine.

He currently is vice-chairman of the government's herbals working group and calls the skeptics who persistently attack him "bullies who have never studied the subjects.

"I'm absolutely convinced that those who look at the map of the sky for the day that they were born and receive some professional guidance will find out a lot about themselves. And it will make their lives easier," he said.

Mr. Tredinnick said he was right about herbal remedies and healing, which are now becoming accepted in parts of the National Health Service (NHS). He now wants to promote astrology, which is "not just about predicting the future but gaining an insight into personal problems."

He stopped short of suggesting astrological readings on the NHS, but said he wanted to raise awareness of it as an alternative among patients and clinicians.

"I think it's something that people should be aware of as an option they have if they are confused about themselves," he said.

"David Tredinnick has shown immense courage and performed a great service in raising this issue, knowing he would face popular misunderstanding that would be fanned by public figures who ought to know better," said Roy Gillett, president of The Astrological Association of Great Britain.

As an example, Gillett cited a popular TV talk show aired in the UK. When commenting on the MP's observations neither of the show's two interviewers or their guests understood that the astrology he was referring to was more than popular newspaper Sun sign columns.

"Sun sign columns are to real astrology as a child playing *Chopsticks* on the piano is to Beethoven's *9th Symphony*. Neither the interviewers nor their guests understood that a chart for the exact moment of birth involves the position of all the planets in all the signs, not just single Sun signs," Gillett said.

"Neither David Tredinnick nor any serious astrologer is suggesting that astrology takes the place of diagnosis or treatment by a qualified medical practitioner. Rather that knowing upcoming pressures in advance can lead to early changes of life-style that avoid illness altogether, or lead to earlier diagnosis and treatment.

"When a problem is unavoidable, a more mindful and positive relationship with the treatment and convalescence afterward may be possible. All of which could save considerable amounts of money as well as easing human suffering.

"With such possibilities available, rather than ridicule astrology with simplistic misinformation we should consider it fully and respectfully," he said.

Getting to Know Pluto Better

By Armand Diaz, PhD

Astrologers look for meaningful correspondences, seeking to find correlations between celestial phenomena and happenings here on earth. While one branch of astrology, *mundane astrology*, is devoted to social and political trends, astrologers are not averse to looking into virtually any realm, even the world of cartoons. The short history of the planet Pluto shows some remarkable similarities to another Pluto, Walt Disney's cartoon dog.

The naming of celestial bodies is not something that involves astrologers—that responsibility falls to astronomers. Whatever the astronomer's proximal reason for naming a planet or asteroid, astrologers assume that there is some thread of meaning running through the process, and that the name will in some way reflect the character, energy, or vibration of the planet. How that works, and how astrology works, is a complex question beyond the scope of this article, but from an astrological perspective it all weaves together pretty well most of the time.

The planet Pluto was named for the Roman god of the underworld, the equivalent of the Greek Hades. In mythology, Pluto is associated with power and wealth (hence the term *Plutocracy*), and bringing up treasures from below. Astrologically, Pluto is associated with the emergence of unconscious contents, as in the psychoanalytic process that was so popular at the time of the planet's discovery in 1930. Pluto is sometimes depicted as the *puer eternis*, the eternal youth, a reflection of the connection between death and rebirth. Ergo, astrologically, Pluto is also associated with deep transformation. As the god of the underworld, Pluto has an appropriately heavy, dangerous sort of reputation in both mythology and astrology.

That Pluto is sometimes seen as a youth is interesting, as the planet was given its name by an eleven year-old girl (her grandfather transmitted the idea to astronomers at the Lowell Observatory, where the planet was discovered). It is perhaps somewhat curious that a young girl should have the Roman god of the underworld on her mind, although young girls do have a place in Plutonian mythology, as the abduction of Propserine by the god and her subsequent rescue by her mother, Ceres, is one of the key myths about Pluto. Astrologers might note that there is a kind of reversal of empowerment in the youth giving the god's name to the planet. In any event, it is not as strange as Disney's decision to name his cartoon dog after the planet, and hence the god.

Walt Disney's own explanation for the naming of the cartoon dog is almost impossibly naïve. He once said: "There was a malaise of humanity sweeping across the country. I decided to take Nate's advice and do something fun and creative. The planet Pluto had recently been discovered and I felt it was appropriate to name the pup in its honor." Was no one in Disney's studio remotely familiar with mythology?

Dogs certainly do have a place in the underworld, but not as the god himself. In Greek and Roman mythology it was Cerberus, the three-headed hellhound, who keeps the dead in the underworld. It is to this fierce guardian figure that Disney's cartoon canine might more appropriately refer. Cerberus has made it into popular culture many times, as in blues singer Robert Johnson's song, *Hellhound on My Trail.*

It is not uncommon for cartoon animals to be anthropomorphized. Something of our human nature is projected onto the animal kingdom in order to make it more palatable to play with images of our human qualities: Bugs Bunny is a slick-talking rabbit, and Daffy Duck is a manic waterfowl. Disney's other cartoon dog, Goofy, is a slightly slow-witted slapstick character.

Interestingly, the cartoon Pluto *is not* anthropomorphized—he remains a dog. He does not talk, dress in human clothing, or otherwise become a person. Perhaps the guardian of the underworld is too powerful a figure to play with, or maybe we are not ready to hear him speak.

In the cartoons, Pluto is Mickey Mouse's pet dog. Now, a mouse might seem like an unlikely cartoon protagonist, although Jerry also fares pretty well in the *Tom and Jerry* cartoons. Our associations with rodents are usually negative. Consider the old taunt, "are you a man or a mouse?" In fact, while the rat is often considered to be treacherous and of dubious moral character, the mouse is a rodent that is frequently associated with meekness—hardly what we would expect for Cerberus' master.

If we dig a bit deeper into the history of Mickey and Pluto, we find a surprising revelation: in the first cartoon in which Pluto appeared, *The Chain Gang* (1930), he is not Mickey's pet dog at all, but is in a role closer to that of Cerberus. He is a bloodhound guarding Mickey, and pursues him when the mouse joins a prison break. In the early cartoons, Mickey is not the good-natured foil that he later became, and in fact he is something of a prankster. After all, some unknown offence landed him on a chain gang. This isn't the mouse we know from his silent handshakes at the Magic Kingdom!

Several reversals have apparently taken place. The meek mouse is the master of the hellhound, who is himself named for the lord of the underworld. The awe-inspiring power of this fearsome god is transferred to a happy cartoon household. It seems that Pluto, known for uncovering difficult truths and bringing them up from the depths, is being hidden in these reversals. We may find it significant that Disney Studios has always been known for its rather clean-cut (some might say sanitized), image. While Warner Brothers characters (Bugs Bunny, Daffy Duck, Road Runner) were often socially and politically edgy, and Max and Dave Fleischer's (Popeye, Betty Boop) could be risqué, Disney produced fare for the American family as wholesome as a moving Norman Rockwell painting.

A very different cartoon character from the underworld is Popeye's nemesis Bluto (an obvious cognate of Pluto). Bluto more overtly represents dark rage, and he shows signs of being self-aware, hence he is represented as a human. It is interesting that he is also sometimes named *Brutus* in the cartoons, suggesting unreasoning stupidity (brute). Thus, Popeye's struggle with Bluto is more overt and far more healing than Mickey's passive adventures with Pluto. Popeye is not a mouse, and so he offers us a more optimistic image, that of the hero who declares, "I am what I am."

While Bluto confronted us with our Plutonian side, Disney's dog led us into a maze of denial and role-reversals, demonstrating that the symbolic energy of Pluto has always been liable to repression and suppression. It is almost as though Disney was intent on telling the world that there was nothing to worry about now that Pluto had made his appearance in the sky. Yet the earliest cartoons featuring 'the pup' belie the image Disney eventually projected. If we dig for the truth—a Plutonian process—we find that even Disney let a little more of the story out than they later recognized.

In 2006, astronomers demoted Pluto to a dwarf planet. Although astrologers have had mixed reactions to this change in status, one popular interpretation has been that the demotion represents an attempt by the collective psyche to repress the energies of Pluto (rather than deal with them constructively), as though seventy-six years of Plutonian awareness was enough. Yet as with the cartoon Pluto—the other Pluto—we can find the truth if we are willing to dig.

Unlikely Import Has Serious Chinese Students Seeing Stars

By Edward Snow

When the claim that there are more than twelve astrological signs in the zodiac reached China's distant shores the reaction was not what you might expect.

According to David Railey, an Atlanta-based astrologer and author who has traveled and lectured extensively in the country, western zodiac signs are popular in China today.

"The controversy created when Minnesota astronomer Parke Kunkle announced that a wobble in the earth's axis had created a new astrological sign immediately lit up the internet blogs and microblogs that comprise China's social media network. Many were confused by the report, which suggested they may not have been born under the astrological influences they thought they were," he said.

But in China the response by at least one influential scientist in a position of authority was unlike anything seen in the western hemisphere. Astronomer Zhu Jin, curator of the prestigious Beijing Planetarium, planned a public discussion of the issue and invited Railey to present astrology's side of the story.

"About half of those in attendance were members of the press who treated the topic like a legitimate news story. We were able to clarify the difference between constellations and astrological signs, but the main discussion focused not on Sun sign astrology but on the kind of serious astrology astronomers in the West rarely bother to learn anything about," he said.

Railey says the event received widespread coverage in the media, including a lengthy story by reporter Youngming Huang that appeared in Southern Weekly, considered by some to be the New York Times of China. At CCTV, the country's national public education station, science and program director Chen Li Hua is working on an educational program that explores the differences between Western and Chinese astrology and astronomy.

Near the end of the Beijing event, Zhu Jin publicly shared his opinion that western astrology "is a beautiful system worthy of further investigation. Astronomers typically take a harder line in other parts of the world," Railey said.

Subject Resonates With Youthful Audience

He points out that the advent of the Internet has coincided with the emergence of a younger, more affluent and well educated Chinese population. There are more than 1.3 billion people in the country and 641 million Internet users with 250 million that read English with fair comprehension.

"A large number have encountered western astrology on the Internet and love it. It speaks to them," he said.

Railey is a past president of the Metro Atlanta Astrological Society and is a member of the steering committee of the Association for Astrological Networking (AFAN)—a group that, among other things, seeks to improve the image of astrology.

His book, *The Soul Purpose*, is published in the Chinese language. A promotional tour arranged by Chinese business partner Felicia Jiang drew large, enthusiastic crowds to lectures, workshops and book signings.

Book sales averaged about 200 copies per day the first month, with the book's first printing selling out after nine months.

"Those attending the lectures were mostly young, 20- to 40-year olds who are wild about astrology. If there were chairs for 60 people there were 90 people standing," he said.

Railey created a blog on Sina, an online Chinese newspaper published in English. By the end of the first year the blog already had been visited by more than 208,000 visitors, and the total has since grown to 979,538, along with a weibo microblog (like twitter) that currently lists 732,910 followers. His name had been Googled in China three and a half million times.

A nodoor.com website posts stories about astrology in the Chinese language, and recently began including news features generated by the Astrology News Service (ANS), an educational news service supported by the major astrological organizations in the United States.

"What's impressive is how serious Chinese students of western astrology are about developing professional standards and taking the necessary steps needed to achieve certification. Obtaining travel visas to study in the United States is not easy for Chinese students, but educational programs have been exported on the Internet and leading U.S. astrologers are finding a receptive audience when they travel to China," he said.

With partner Felicia Jiang, Raily founded a school for astrology in China that in 2014 had grown to 500 students throughout the country. The school received certification from the International Society for Astrological Research (ISAR) in 2013.

About the Authors

Steven Forrest
Steven has been working as an astrologer professionally for more than 40 years and has written several classic best-selling astrology books. He has traveled the globe teaching a practical and transformative style of astrology. And he is committed to practicing his own style of responsible, inspiring, choice-centered astrology. More articles and information about the author can be found at forrestastrology.com.

Grant Lewi
Grant Lewi (1902-1951) The late Grant Lewi achieved something most astrological writers only dream of. Lewi received a graduate degree from Columbia University and went on to teach English at Dartmouth College and other universities before leaving academia to become an astrologer and the writer of two best-selling books on the subject, Astrology for the Millions and Heaven Knows What. This article first published in Astrology for the Millions, which after 60 years can still be purchased at amazon.com.

Dorothy Oja
Dorothy Oja is a certified astrological professional (ISAR-CAP) who offers individual consultations through her practice, MindWorks. She is an active writer for national magazines and online sites. For the past 17 years she has published a bi-monthly newsmagazine—PlanetWeather, which includes social, cultural and political commentary. Her first book, *Planetary Resonance, Everything Leaves a Trace*, was released in May 2012. She currently serves as Chair of ISAR's Ethics Awareness Training and ISAR's Ethics Mediation Committee. She also serves on the Advisory Council for ANS. More information is available at her website, planetweather.net, and her FB page: planetweathernews. Contact: DOja07@gmail.com

Edward Snow
Edward Snow is Managing Editor of the Astrology News Service (ANS). He is a former news reporter and publicist and has been a student of astrology for many years.

Adrian Ross Duncan

Adrian Ross Duncan is a full-time practicing astrologer. For seven years he was both president of the Copenhagen Astrological association (Ekliptika) and ran AstrologSkolen, a finishing school for consultant astrologers. He is the author of Doing Time on Planet Earth and Astrology: Transformation and Empowerment. More information on the author is available at the world-of-wisdom.com website.

Robert Gover

Robert Gover grew up in an endowed orphanage in Philadelphia, received a BA from the University of Pittsburgh in economics, became a best-selling novelist at age 30, lived most of his life in California and now lives in a Delaware beach community. He has published eight novels plus other works of fiction and nonfiction. A new edition of his most famous novel, One Hundred Dollar Misunderstanding, has been published by Hopewell Publications. He began studying astrology in the 1960s and in the 1980s he combined astrology with economics to research planetary cycles that repeat with economic cycles. You can find more information at: http://robert-gover.blogspot.com.

Richard Tarnas

Richard Tarnas, PhD, is a cultural historian and professor of philosophy and depth psychology at the California Institute of Integral Studies in San Francisco, where he is founding director of the Philosophy, Cosmology and Consciousness graduate program. His first book, The Passions of the Western Mind, is required reading at many Universities. At the website for his second book, www.cosmosandpsyche.com, he provides an in-depth description of the archetypal forces and the planetary "aspects" that impact them. More information is available at the cosmosandpsyche.com website.

Diana K Rosenberg

The late Diana Rosenberg was the astrological community's leading authority on Fixed Stars and devoted her life to research and recovery of the most ancient roots of sky knowledge. An NCGR certified professional astrologer, she formerly was Vice President of NCGR's Uranian Society and Copy Editor of the NCGR Journal. She has written articles for many astrological magazines and journals and is the author of a Fixed Star Workbook and Encyclopedia of Fixed Stars and Constellations. She also is the author of Secrets of the Ancient Skies: Fixed Stars and Constellations in Natal and Mundane Astrology. More information is at http://ye-stars.com.

Glenn Perry

Glenn Perry, PhD, MAT is an ISAR certified astrological professional (CAP) and a licensed psychotherapist in Haddam Neck, CT. In addition to private practice, Dr. Perry is director of the Academy of AstroPsychology, an online school that offers courses and training in psychological astrology. Glenn has written eight books, including An Introduction to AstroPsychology, and serves as a Board member and qualitative research advisor for ISAR. He lectures internationally on the application of astrology to the fields of counseling and psychotherapy. His website is aaperry.com.

Nick Kollerstrom

Nick Kollerstrom, PhD, is a science historian and former honorary research fellow in Science and Technology Studies at University College, London (UCL). He is the author of several books, including Gardening and Planting by the Moon and Farmers Moon, a thorough investigation of scientific evidence linking waxing and waning cycles to farming and gardening. He is a former gardening correspondent for the BBC and, over the years, has published numerous articles in scientific and astrological publications.

Robert Currey

Robert Currey, BSc.[Hons], D.F.Astrol.S., Cert.ACG.Int. has been a professional astrologer since 1981. While working as a consultant, he wrote a series of astrology software programs. He marketed the resulting interpretations through his company Equinox and later through the Astrology Shop in London, which he founded in 1981. His specialty is Astro*Carto*Graphy and Equinox holds the license to print A*C*G world maps. Besides consulting, he is involved in writing, lecturing and research. He has written a series of peer reviewed papers for Correlation Journal and is science editor for the Astrology News Service.

Frank Piechoski

Frank Piechoski has been studying astrology for virtually his entire life—some of his first reading material was astrology-oriented. He holds a degree from the University of Wisconsin-Madison in both journalism (news editorial) and theatre (acting specialist). He is apt to lose himself in both historical and quantitative research at any given moment. He is active in numerous astrology groups and organizations and lectures internationally.

John Marchesella

A professional astrologer since 1976, John Marchesella is NCGR-PAA certified. He is the current Chair of NCGR and has written numerous columns for popular magazines and websites, such as HomeStore.com and AstroToGo.com. He is a contributor to Under One Sky, an innovative anthology on astrological approaches. In addition to his astrological credentials he is a bereavement counselor and certified psychotherapist. More information can be found at his website, astrojohn.com.

John Townley

John Townley is a pioneer astrologer, musician, journalist, and maritime historian. He was certified by the Astrological Guild of America in 1972 and is the "father" of the composite chart, an astrological technique he introduced in 1973. His lifelong work with astrological and natural cycles has long been oriented toward a better delineation of the physical basis for astrology. Current books include The Composite Chart, Lunar Returns, Dynamic Astrology, and Planets In Love. Other articles by the author can be found at the www.astrococktail.com website

Armand Diaz

Armand M. Diaz, PhD, is a consciousness researcher and NCGR certified counseling astrologer (Level IV) with a doctorate from the California Institute of Integral Studies. He is articles editor and writes book reviews for ANS and is the author of Integral Astrology: Understanding the Ancient Discipline in the Contemporary World and other books. More information can be found on his website, integralastrology.net.